To all my friends at APS
For your help
   With love and gratitude
      Marta Marchisan
        September 30, 2005

Learning Disabilities: The Myth

By

Marta L Marchisan, Ph D

1663 LIBERTY DRIVE, SUITE 200
BLOOMINGTON, INDIANA 47403
(800) 839-8640
www.AuthorHouse.com

The author wishes to express her deepest gratitude to L. Ron Hubbard, author, humanitarian, and educator, without whose writings on study technology and the human spirit, spanning more than half a century, she never could have solved the riddle in teaching students with disabilities. This data helped her understand what she knows and to explain it in this book.

This book is a work of non-fiction. Names of people and places have been changed to guarantee privacy. The views stated are those of the author and do not necessarily represent the views of DOD or its components.

© 2005 Marta L Marchisan, Ph D. All Rights Reserved.

No part of this book may be reproduced, stored in a retrieval system, or transmitted by any means without the written permission of the author.

First published by AuthorHouse 06/21/05

ISBN: 1-4184-5653-5 (e)
ISBN: 1-4184-5654-3 (sc)
ISBN: 1-4184-5655-1 (dj)

Library of Congress Control Number: 2004096746

Printed in the United States of America
Bloomington, Indiana

This book is printed on acid-free paper.

For Karl Heinz Gross and Margret Weissmüller

Table of Contents

Introduction ix
The Myth 1
Drugs as an Aide to Learning 10
Sorting and Dividing 22
IQ Can Be Raised 32
On Behavior 38
On Observation 50
On Reading 53
On Writing 61
On Math 78
On Communication 83
Establishing Control 92
Tips for Managing the Classroom 112
Application 129
On Understanding 132
What the Teacher Confronts 137
The Student as a Spiritual Being 149

Introduction

I have seen education from the top down and the bottom up as a graduate assistant supervising student teachers, and as a teacher in preschool. I have worked with students of all ages, in elementary school, middle school, and high school, both in regular education and in special education. Working with these different populations and disabilities, I have found that all these students have the same needs but learn at different rates. Children are labeled and considered disabled by an education system that is suppressive and has lost touch with its teachers and its students. The system labels children as an excuse for not knowing and applying the correct technology. When the correct technology is applied, one can learn anything.

I got tired of the exploitation in special education. Again and again, I saw students who did not belong but only needed to learn how to learn. That was the biggest problem of the majority of students that I worked with in the resource room. There were many regular education students who had problems and who could have benefited from the help, but could not get it. There were students whose parents exploited special education and convinced their child that "something was wrong" with him. What these parents wanted was someone to make their lazy child do his homework because they were too burned-out to do it. There were teachers who were frustrated, and lacked the time and energy to deal with the *one,* when they had a class full of students who needed to be taught. There was the coach who used the handicap of a student to gain publicity for his basketball team. There was the counselor who just wanted to get the student graduated, regardless of whether he learned anything or not. There was the administrator who used the special education guidance to discipline a teacher. There was the special education teacher who did paperwork and did not teach because paperwork was what was valued. There was the psychologist who loved to baffle everyone with the latest diagnosis from the DSM manual, but never had a workable plan. There was the psychiatrist who drugged students based on little more than an interview with the student and family, and check sheets from the teacher.

I saw millions of dollars spent on equipment, kits and gimmicks, teacher training for procedures, all designed to fix the problem. I saw teachers burn out and quit education altogether. I saw grade inflation, where course material was not learned but credit given. And now my system plans to improve learning by spending $56.5 million over the next six years. They plan to increase paraprofessional hours and provide support for assessment, buy more equipment, and train some more. Yet I have seen nothing on looking at the student and nothing on learning to teach the student. I learned that teaching students with learning problems was invalidating, because there was too little gain over too long a period. I learned that most teachers wanted to help the student with disabilities, but did not know how.

For these reasons and for all the students that I have taught over the years, I write this book. I write this book to show that there is hope, that there is a way out of this hypocrisy and illiteracy that we have created in education. I write this book to show that we can fix the problem!

The Myth

What is a learning disability? The definition depends on where you live or teach. Although there is a standard textbook definition, there is considerable debate and little acceptance over what officially constitutes a learning disability, and this has led to over-identification and excessive labeling of students. The criteria for admission to special education programs differ from one part of the country to another. Even the title of the person who teaches this population may differ. Therefore, a student in one state may not be eligible in another. Psychologists, psychiatrists, and special education teachers sometimes could not understand what the learning disability was and, as a result, could not establish a workable plan. Because of its complexities, the technical language used excluded others, especially regular-classroom teachers and parents. Thus, lawyers who specialize in this field were called in to sort through all the language and regulations. This led to a constant stream of ever changing procedures and paperwork that smothered the special education teacher. It set up barriers for anyone who wanted to teach the student. And the student was ignored as far as educating him was concerned. There were a lot of unanswered questions. Why did all this have to be so complicated? What was the basic problem? Why could not a student with average intelligence learn?

Learning disabilities, like education, had not been defined adequately, and everyone got lost in all the significance. It was too complex, too theoretical. Every endeavor to simplify the process netted more and more paperwork. Mountains of it! Mix in disgruntled parents, lawyers and politicians, and you have a game of chaos. The game caused regular inspection of records and forms. Documentation reigned supreme. Documentation of what? Our failure as a society? The student over here wants to learn, so why did teaching him have to be so complicated? No one knew that education meant application, and students with learning disabilities, above all, desperately needed to apply what they learned. So I learned early on to ignore what I could and attempted to address the problems of learning.

No one looked at the student to see how he learned. Someone could not figure out how to teach a particular student for one reason or another and decided something must be wrong with him. They convinced themselves and the education hierarchy that he could not learn unless severe measures were taken. Severe measures were taken, and these measures have cost taxpayers millions of dollars and teachers untold hours of paperwork and meetings, with little benefit to the student. Hordes of specialists were called in to meet the student's needs that had been identified by other specialists and were, subsequently, addressed on the individualized educational plans (IEPs). By the time the student was evaluated, counseled, and staffed, he had adopted the "learned helplessness" syndrome so prevalent among many. He had lost all control over his education, and his own purpose dimmed. His parents became believers in the *myth* that something was indeed wrong with their child and were somewhat relieved that they had not directly caused this disability. These individualized programs then perpetuated the myth and sometimes led to disagreements among staff, specialists, parents, and students, and still the student got no better. Why? He believed that something was wrong with him.

Nothing from my university days prepared me for what I would find in the classroom. What I needed to know, I had to find out on my own, and the answers were not found in the textbooks I had studied, *or* from the meetings I had attended. I had to devise methods of survival teaching as I began my career, equipped with all the credentials and very little else but intention. I would find out what I needed to know by observing my students and letting them guide me. The students would be my teacher. Just looking at student behaviors gave the answer every time. Therefore, I became very adept at observation and devising an immediate plan. I started to ignore the labels altogether. I dutifully typed up the fiction from the experts, presented it to determine eligibility, and then checked off the canned IEP goals. It never mattered what was printed off, signed, and distributed. What did matter, and mattered a great deal, was what was going on in the actual instructional phase. My intention was that the student would learn and flourish. Generally, he did. This led me to the conclusion that learning disability was only a label that could be misapplied to just about anyone. When taught properly, all could learn, all could retain, and all could apply.

Learning Disabilities: The Myth

During my teaching career, I have had the opportunity to read hundreds of case files on students with about any label you can imagine. There were many discrepancies from one report to another. A student could be disabled in one state and suddenly cured in another. Repeatedly, there was remarks like: "This kid is borderline IQ," or "This student can't read and is making all F's," or "He can do the work when he chooses." There was very little agreement on anything concerning the learning disability diagnosis, no reality about the problem. So how could anything get fixed? As I examined the achievement profiles, I saw a trend emerge: nearly all had reading deficits. I figured that the reading could be corrected if I were to analyze exactly what the student's deficit was and remedy at that point. The majority of the students with severe reading problems had very low decoding scores that were explained away by terms like auditory processing or short-term memory deficits. Another problem was that those students who could decode the words did not fully understand many of the words they had read. They would always fly by the words they did not know and sink deeper and deeper into non-comprehension.

Any educational plan only works when the child is recognized as the spiritual being that he is. The student is a spirit apart from his mind and body. And as a spirit, the student has infinite potential and is capable of learning and progressing in school. He is *not* a stimulus-robot machine with fixed ability for life. The spirit as defined in *Second College Edition: The American Heritage Dictionary*, (1991, Houghton Mifflin Co.) is the vital principle or animating force traditionally believed to be within living beings. It is the élan vital. As a spirit, the student must be given some measure of self-determinism over his own learning. Special education teachers have the capacity and desire to help these students, as do most teachers. They try everything to help them survive in school with modifications such as: extra tutoring sessions, reduction of assignments, extra time, retake tests for grade improvement, modified tests and so forth. The failure cycle may end for a while, but none of these modifications helps the student be a better student so that he can use this data. The steep gradient of the curriculum with its multitude of unknown words defeats all efforts to make the learning stick. Often, the student moves away, gets a new school and new teachers, and the cycle of failure starts again, unless he is extraordinarily lucky. Then the process of identification, testing and staffing begin anew. Those that do make it are at risk in their professions due to misunderstood words and reading problems that plagued them throughout school. A few of the more successful students do become teachers, doctors, and lawyers and enter other well-paid professions; some carry with them their baggage of misunderstood words. No matter the changes in the law, the cycle of not knowing, not understanding, and stupidity continues for the majority.

The permissiveness of the last decades in education has led us to a general decline in the classroom. When teachers, also the product of a suppressive education system, cannot come together on what it is we want students to do and then model it faithfully, we have problems, almost insurmountable. The special education teacher, being at the lowest end of the pecking order, took the student from the "experts" and tried to make something of him. Together with the regular class teacher, she tried to make a workable plan. For the most part, it was up to her to figure everything out. Usually she did, despite the limitations and lack of real assistance. Sometimes the IEP worked and the student made it, but mostly he did not. The experts wanted to be consultants and said it was this or that thing or the other, but it was the special education teacher who was always the *plan* of these experts. The regular teacher was very dependent on the special education teacher. She wanted the special education teacher to either pull him out of the class and teach him, or make the special education plan work in her class with the minimum of effort, and no basic changes in the teaching technology. These students at the low end of the learning curve are, by this time in high school, sources of trouble for themselves and those around them. It takes the strong intention of a teacher with good control to turn them around. It takes a teacher who acknowledges that they are spirits, and who has a certainty that they can learn. It takes a teacher who conveys that there is hope.

In the beginning the goal was to get the students with learning disabilities into vocational programs or the military; today, the goal is to prepare them *all* for college. In recent years, all my students planned to go to college. They say it is their goal. They say this because that is what their peers and the middle class tell them. Few make it. Consequently, the practice of pulling them out of most of their regular classes changed to putting them all back into those classes. Neither extreme worked. Modifying classes got them through the curriculum, but it rarely made a better student, one who knows and can apply what he knows. And as a result, we are still graduating illiterates! And some go into education! One such student (not illiterate but loaded with misunderstood words and concepts), son of a colleague, visited me during his Christmas break. He is a very likeable young man with a great sense of humor. His plan is to become a physical education teacher and do some counseling. His mother is pushing him in this direction. Most likely, he will be employed as a teacher and pass on his ignorance. He has the potential to be a very good teacher if he would be willing to learn how to study, and then do it. In the majority of cases, a year or so following graduation, most of these students are still at risk for being unemployed. Why? They never were checked to see if they could apply what they had learned. We automatically assume that students already know how to learn, and we admonish them by saying, "Study harder!" They leave school with reading, writing, and math deficits that are not likely to be corrected. Even sadder, few have marketable skills unless they have been highly trained in some good vocational programs. A student who had survived the rigorous curriculum in our system wrote, "I'm pushing carts for Wal-Mart. People get on my nerves... I might work in a factory." She never had an opportunity to apply job skills outside the classroom in a vocational program, and she never had a communication course. In the last fifteen years or so, all vocation classes have been dropped from the curriculum. Now our system is gearing up for high tech computer courses, yet these courses overwhelm students at the lower quartile.

By the time the student identified as having disabilities arrives in high school, he is apathetic about learning, and the parents and teachers are exhausted from dealing with him. He presents his body only and may become a discipline problem—a problem to himself and others. He has no agreement about being in school to learn, no affinity for the courses and materials of study, and cannot follow the language of instruction. Add to that years of frustration with no application and we have an unmotivated learner, a disorganized learner, and one who has no interest in solving his learning problems. He is not present because he does not understand or agree to help; will not allow himself to be controlled, and, therefore, cannot control things himself; cannot communicate with the subject matter and his teachers fully; and has lost all hope. No matter what the experts say about auditory processing, visual processing, or processing speed, the problem got started when the student got hung up on something he did not understand.

Twenty-five years ago I thought I knew what was going on in my field of teaching; I did not. Little did I realize that every year thereafter, the forms would change, the procedures would change, and even my title and the category of the student would change. Paperwork piled higher and deeper. No matter how hard you tried, you never got it right. The student never changed, but he grew more apathetic about learning, for often he was ignored as far as individualized teaching went, once he demonstrated that he could not understand. He became a behavior problem, or sat in a stupor of non-comprehension, or became a glib student who memorized data to pass the tests. No one ever looked at the student and what really prevented him from learning. Instead, the education and psychology departments at the universities looked at characteristics and created more interesting labels or improved the old ones. Nothing was in place to teach the student how to learn.

I determined that these students could learn if the gradient and rate of learning were correct. They could progress if they understood what they learned and could demonstrate it. The lie that was perpetuated in special education was that learning problems could **not** be fixed. The wisdom handed down was that students with learning disabilities had something wrong with them and, therefore, they better learn to compensate. They should learn to compensate because these deficits were inherent in the individual. They would grow up and still have these disabilities, so the special education teacher's job was to teach them survival skills and insure that regular-class teachers made proper modifications of the curriculum. Everyone from the university on down bought into this because no

Learning Disabilities: The Myth

one had figured out the real problem. The professors writing the textbooks on methodology had not discovered that students needed to *learn how to learn.*

I have a responsibility to share what I have found to increase literacy on this planet. Improving literacy is simple, and complex laws do not need to be written and enforced for students to learn. We spend so much time discussing characteristics, procedures, and labels of handicaps, that we become overwhelmed. Then we lose our purpose! We are burned out before we begin. None of this esoteric talk has ever made a bit of difference in the way that I taught students. It did not help me teach them, nor did it help them learn better. Most of us know our subject matter but not always how to teach it effectively. This is because the education system has made it all too complex. This is the reason we become bogged down.

I tell my students; "There is nothing wrong with you! Someone said there was, but there is not." There is nothing wrong with the majority of students placed in mild to moderate special education programs when they do not keep the same pace as their peers. They have misunderstood their purpose for being in school. No one has told them that all this learning is for application, and so they are hung up at the very entrance to learning. They can learn and improve their rate of learning and increase their intelligence. With the postulate that there is nothing wrong with them, it becomes easy to teach those labeled as learning disabled. First, we must establish what our purpose is and remember who we are teaching—a human spirit with infinite potential, not a stimulus-response robot. The role of the teacher is to help the student establish his purpose and teach him *how* to study. The student then learns how to correct his own learning problems. He becomes self-determined.

In the beginning, my techniques of teaching were not as well-oiled and polished as they are today, but I grew with my students over the years and found ways to do my job better and teach those the system had despaired of teaching. The message handed down was patch it up and get them graduated. But I wanted more than that; I wanted them to be able to learn and apply what they learned, otherwise they would be a burden to themselves and society later on. I knew that they could learn if I could find a way. I did. I discovered

Study Technology developed by L. Ron Hubbard some forty years ago. He identified the three barriers to study that are explained in his *Basic Study Manual* and courses based on his works offered at Applied Scholastics International. He also explains some of the major physiological and mental symptoms that accompany each of the barriers. Study Technology is the method that I use in my classroom to teach students. It works extremely well, hampered only by the burdensome significance that exists in our school system's curriculum. I was already applying much of his technology and basic principles as a spiritual being because they seemed right, yet without knowing why. Hubbard helped me understand what I know and why what I did worked. When I discovered why, it was a tremendous validation of what I was doing correctly in the classroom. I came to understand and describe what I had learned about teaching these students. Not only was I able to teach students better, I am now able to explain why these methods are effective. The student with learning disabilities suffers from *too steep of a study gradient* and almost always has some deficit in reading, from mild to severe. He has *misunderstood words* and concepts that he was allowed to pass by, and he *lacked the mass* when needed to demonstrate understanding. We all recognize these barriers, though we may call them by something else. The problem is: we, in education, never had a workable plan to remedy these barriers. These barriers got mixed in with everything else that the psychologists, psychiatrists, and specialists were telling us to do.

The field of special education is burdensome with its process of identification, testing, meetings and reams of paperwork. It is loaded with specialists, consultants and complex theories of the origins of the problems. It is sparse in a workable technology for learning, if learning is our goal. Using Hubbard's technology, I was able to refine what I was doing and explain the success of my students. His technology is simple, direct, and it works—if applied correctly and with precision. It can simplify the overwhelming data in this field that suppresses the teacher in her quest to teach. Students can overcome their learning disability with the application of this technology and when they are recognized as spirits with infinite potential. When I applied Hubbard's methods, my understanding

Learning Disabilities: The Myth

of what I knew increased, and so did the success of my students. Their rate of learning soared, and I watched students progress up the gradient of learning.

The idea that a learning disability exists is a myth, a myth that has been established by an education system and government that is completely out of touch with what is happening in the classroom. It is a lot of dead talk perpetrated by special interest groups and has grown to unmanageable proportions and overwhelming costs. It is a myth that is laying waste to some of our brightest students who were never taught to read. This myth is sinking us as a society because our future is at stake. This myth is perpetuating illiteracy in our Western nations, who should know better. These nations, given their resources, should be leading the rest of the world in eradicating illiteracy, not contributing to it. The choice is ours; we can choose to sink our society or salvage it. It is already late!

Drugs as an Aide to Learning

Drugs do not aide learning; drugs make zombies out of students and inhibit their learning to a marked degree. A student may stay in his seat longer and talk out less, but he is not learning. It may even cause the teacher to praise his behavior and remark on his improved concentration, but he still is not learning. He may even be completing some assignments that are done by rote or glibness, but he is not learning. In some instances, his marks may improve due to what is perceived as good effort by the teacher. His personality has changed, and he is almost in a semi-conscious state of awareness.

Students are spiritual beings, and adding drugs not only complicates learning, it makes it impossible for the student to observe and record accurately. Observation is the foundation of learning, and drugs dull the senses. Teachers, psychologists, and student assistant teams, frustrated at their own inability to fix the problem, have relied heavily on the medical establishment for answers. The proliferation of drugs in our society is generated through the persistence of the psychiatric and medical establishment. Without a workable plan in place that can aide student learning, they turn to the only plan they know: prescribing drugs. This appears to be a quick fix, when in fact it is a slow kill. Once the student is drugged, he is at risk for sure. The drugs do not work, and the student generally does not like the effects of the drugs, nor do his parents. The psychologists in the schools heavily enforce this drug-addiction craze by suggesting that the student take his medication or, if not on any, refer the student to the psychiatrists or other medical doctors with the intention that the student be medicated.

The major source of student data comes in the form of check sheets filled out by the individual teachers of the student. This scanty bit of information plus what the parent provides is often all that is required to get a diagnosis of Attention Deficit Hyperactive Disorder (ADHD) and a drug prescription. In my school, for example, the data for an ADHD referral consist of, at best, two to three completed check sheets, accompanied by remarks from the referring person and the sanction of the parent, who is all too happy to get this student off the failure roster and the school off his back. With this information in hand, the psychiatrist then has an interview with the student and parent and prescribes medication—Ritalin, Cylert, Adderall, or whatever for the ADHD. The Emotionally Impaired label is fairly easy to come by and this student, too, is offered drugs. Teachers are pleased because peace is restored to their classrooms, if nothing else, and at least this in-seat and out-of-seat activity of the ADHD student is not wrecking havoc with the rest of the class. For a period of time, the medicine appears to work, maybe even the student's grades improve, but at what price? For many, this does not work. It leads to aggressive behavior, and once the student is taken off the medicine, he is right back where he was, and the worse for having had the experience. Perhaps, we got better production temporarily, but we did not get a better student.

I have observed dozens of students who were on drugs prescribed by psychiatrists for ADHD and anti-depressants for the so-called suicidal and emotionally impaired students. I read their case histories, talk to their parents, and interview them. Oh, they *will* stay in their seats and give the teacher a much-needed break, but what is the exchange? I have watched their stares and blank expressions **after** these dosages of behavior controlling drugs. They are quiet and they are pretending to work. I have seen students refuse the drugs because of its effect on them, only to be cajoled by the psychologist or nurse into taking the drug because it is so "beneficial" to them. These students are being invalidated and suppressed in one form or another. These are problems that could be corrected.

Hawking drugs to school age students is big business, a profitable business. Recently, I learned that in the state of Virginia many of the elementary schools had lines for Ritalin during lunch that were longer than the lines for lunch only. About the same time, I opened a recent copy of *Reader's Digest*, a family magazine that has been around for years and prides itself in offering wholesome advice, and saw two advertisements for drugs for ADHD. One showed a charming young boy, about eight years old, wearing a baseball cap backwards, sitting on a stoop with a baseball mitt on one hand, with the caption: "Already Done with my Homework Dad." Underneath this picture is an ad: "Adderall XR all-day symptom control in a single daily dose. Works fast for the start of the school day—with or without food. Helps improve academic performance." In smaller print, it states that the most common side effects are decreased appetite, stomachache, difficulty falling asleep, and emotional lability. A few pages over in the same magazine is an ad for a competitor, Concerta. This page shows a smiling preteen of about twelve, with his mother. Concerta advertises higher scores when solving math problems, overall improved classroom focus, and fewer conflicts among adolescents with family members and friends. It also lists in smaller print that the most common side effects are headache, stomach pain, sleeplessness, and decreased appetite. Then on the next page, with the same smiling preteen and mother, it offers a scholarship contest for three age groups: 6–9, 10–13, and 14–18 years old. The caption reads, "I See Success—ADHD Scholarship Contest."

The media has a powerful influence on what the middle class thinks and does. In an effort to do the right thing and follow the doctor's orders and the school's recommendations, a law-abiding citizen can get rather confused and stay that way until it is too late almost to salvage his own child. Films featuring super-stars like Dustin Hoffman as an ADHD adult who needs his medication right away to function, and cartoons such as "Finding Nemo" with Dori, the fish with a short-term memory loss, appeal to the masses and all contribute to the need for labeling and drugs. Advertising has a snowball effect and can create an avalanche of misinformation.

Today, more and more students are being identified as handicapped and placed into special education programs all over the country because the current education system is lacking the technology to teach these students. As the push by society for a university degree increases, so does the rigor of the high school curriculum as a preparatory step. Any student is at risk for being labeled! The medical establishment, especially psychiatrists and clinical psychologists, add to this mushrooming problem with labels of ADHD and emotional impairment of one description or another. Primarily, these students have behavior problems resulting from a communication break with learning, or something basic that they have misunderstood. They do not belong in special education, and, certainly, not on Ritalin or any other drug. There is now a growing debate about placing such children on drugs. The behaviors must be

Learning Disabilities: The Myth

corrected so that learning can take place for sure, but administering drugs is not the answer.

"The psychiatrist does not do any testing. The psychiatrist listens to the history and then prescribes a drug," states Dr. Mary Ann Block, author of *No More ADHD*. I can verify this quote as the absolute truth in my dealings with referrals of the so-called ADHD cases in my school system. The behavior management specialist, a special education teacher, passes around the ACTeRS Teacher Form (Copyright 1991 by Metri Tech, Inc., Champaign, Illinois) and C. Keith Conners' Teacher Rating Scale—Revised (L) to teachers of a supposedly learning disabled student, collects these forms (often the return is only one or two), and passes them on to the clinic, where a clinical psychologist reads and diagnoses the student as having ADHD or forwards his findings to the psychiatrist. The psychiatrist listens to the history, pronounces the student ADHD, and then prescribes the Ritalin or whatever drug he deems appropriate. The plan is almost always drugs and referral to special education, with the student qualifying under "Other Health Impaired." The special education teacher has to get the behavior problems under control to do any good. The drug may make the student calmer and more zombie-like, but does not assist learning. Some students already have severe learning problems, and the ADHD comes as a second diagnosis. To date, I have never dealt with a student diagnosed as primary or secondary ADHD who did not have a behavior problem brought on by misunderstood words. Generally, that is *the* problem. At the core of the behavior problem was always a mild to severe reading comprehension problem or a decoding problem, or both. Sometimes there were allergies and sleep problems causing an inability to focus. Almost always the student lacked motivation to learn and was no longer self-determined about the learning. He would not do his homework or complete class work, if he had started it at all. Often with a little homework supervision and reading intervention, this student got better unless he was drugged. A few students suffered only from no control or bad control at home.

Dr. Mary Ann Block, who became a doctor after her daughter's physical problems were treated with psychiatric drugs asks: "If there is no valid test for ADHD, no data proving ADHD is a brain dysfunction, no long-term studies of the drugs' effects and if the drugs do not improve academic performance or social skills and the drugs can cause compulsive and mood disorders and can lead to illicit drug use, why in the world are millions of children, teenagers and adults being labeled with ADHD and prescribed these drugs?"

What are the facts?

- The childhood use of mind-altering drugs is a major contributing factor to later cocaine dependence. (Nadine Lambert, Director, School Psychology Program, University of California-Berkeley Graduate School of Education, Report to National Institute of Health, news release May 5, 1999.)
- Studies show that children who take amphetamine-type or other prescribed, mind-altering drugs do not perform better academically. In fact, children who take these drugs fail just as many courses and drop out of school just as often as children who did not take the drugs (p. 53. N. Lambert).

All these unnatural chemicals from modern society contribute to inhibiting children's perceptions. The biggest offender of drug overdose in schools today is the prescription of Ritalin and similar drugs to control hyperactivity after a diagnosis of Attention Deficit Hyperactivity Disorder. While I have seen it make zombies out of children, I have never seen it contribute to learning. What I have observed is that it alters their mood, keeps them in their seat, and controls them. There is no evidence of an increase in retention or learning rate, yet many teachers and parents swear by it.

However, there *is* evidence to suggest that the residual effects of these drugs linger long past the point where the drug was discontinued. Just as the student suffers from flashbacks and tremors years later from the use of marijuana and other illegal drugs, so does he suffer from the lingering effects of legal ones. Drugs make it next to impossible to teach the student. Why? Because he is no longer self-determined.

The only plan that psychiatrists have for students that they diagnose as ADHD is drugs. Their bible, the DSM manual (American Psychiatric Association Diagnostic and Statistical Manual of Mental Disorders), has grown from only fifty-nine forms of mental disorders

Learning Disabilities: The Myth

in 1917 to 106 disorders in 1952, and now the latest version of the manual lists 292 possible diagnoses, from "Major Depression" and "Schizophrenia" to designations like "Hypoactive Sexual Desire Disorder." In Eric Goode's article, "Sick or just quirky?" (*U.S. News & World Report,* 10 February 1992), he suggests that perhaps the multiplicity of mental disorders has gone too far. For instance, fifty years ago no one considered smoking cigarettes abnormal, but DSM III included "Nicotine Dependence." The "Self-Defeating Personality Disorder" is defined as someone who "enters into relationships with persons or places himself in situations that are self-defeating and have painful consequences." This disorder was placed in the appendix, following objections from critics. Goode writes that the present system "does more to obscure patients' problems than to clarify them."

The latest diagnosis to capture the attention of special education coordinators in my system is "Asperger's Syndrome" listed in the Diagnostic Statistical Manual IV of Mental Disorders (DSM IV Text Revision, 2000). This child is described as having average to superior intellectual capacity, looks typical but lacks the social awareness to connect with his world. They were referred to as "little professors" in the article by the *experts* that I read. These children are described as preoccupied with a narrow interest and may move into the personal space of others. When I finished the article, I still did not know what the syndrome was, yet I was cautioned to be on the lookout, and reminded that this growing awareness would lead to significantly increased identification. You bet it will! See, this is part of the game. Slowly but surely, we are categorizing everyone. Some people enjoy working alone more than they do in groups. What is wrong with that? Talk about group responsibility and offer opportunities for group participation, but do not automatically assume that the little professor is messed up. The right group for the individual must be considered and the right match to insure understanding. Otherwise, why work in a group if the participants cannot come to agreement, have effective communication and build some affinity for one another. Perhaps, his vocabulary and ideas are considerably advanced for the group. The gradient may be too steep to plop this student into any group and expect only bare tolerance for differences. He needs communication training, as do all. And he needs constructed opportunities to succeed with the right group and alone, but that does not mean that he has a mental illness. Do we want a society of look-alike, act-alike robots?

As you can see, just about any human experience not considered ideal is at risk for being labeled and placed in the DSM manual. In fact, there are so many types of mental illnesses that none of us is free. Think about it for a minute, those who are making all these labels are not free from the labels themselves, nor are the teachers required to teach these labeled students. All qualify for the labels! We become fixed on these labels and say that the student must learn to cope. So we are getting ourselves into a stew, aren't we? Who is left that is normal according to this manual? It used to be that the degree and intensity of a specified behavior made it normal or abnormal. Who knows anymore. This is the reason I choose to ignore this fiction when I work with my students. Labels themselves stick to a person and create enormous barriers in life, so I always tell them that there is nothing wrong with them. I tell them that we can do something to correct the learning problem which is invariably something not understood. I convey to my students the intention that they will succeed, and it is powerful. It is so powerful that I have seen students turn around from not doing to doing. Sometimes, it might take a year and a half, but it happens.

A student that I had for exactly a year and a half did nothing, I mean absolutely nothing. During his ninth grade year, I leaned on him constantly in a step-by-step approach with nearly every single subject. I could tell he suffered from the "Mommy Do It Syndrome," but I felt like I had to do something to help. All the while, I was checking to see if he would initiate anything independently. He was a nice looking boy, adored by the girls and his mother, very polite and never a minute of trouble in class. Only he would not produce anything in the absence of the teacher and in the past, his mother. What was the problem? A psychiatrist had labeled him with the very vague ADHD diagnosis. Without help, he was failing miserably, yet very able. The second year, I decided to let him fail but was always available to offer assistance when he reached for it. I probably was not very popular on the home front the first quarter when he got a

Learning Disabilities: The Myth

couple of F's and a D. When the quarter marks came out, I called each student in for a conference. Each time, if the marks were low, I asked them what they could do about it, and this boy was no exception. I showed him with colored blocks how I overcame obstacles to achieve a particular goal. One day a short time later, I gave an example of how I saw all this learned helplessness get started. I illustrated this with a true example of the child of a friend of mine. This boy said in front of the class, "That sounds like me." Before long, he was making A's in all three classes without a shred of assistance. He no longer needed extra help or extra time or anything. He stopped by my desk one day after class and said a "doctor", presumably a psychiatrist, had said something was wrong with him. I asked him, "Is there anything wrong with you?" He replied very forcefully, "No!" I said, "Good! I agree." He had been labeled ADHD about three years before and given a prescription for Ritalin. Afterwards, he had become fixed on that label and given up, but now, he was self-determined. Why? Because he found that nothing was wrong with himself and that he could do something about his learning. This was a miracle! (Actually, this should be routine.)

The public has begun to challenge the diagnosis of Attention Deficit Hyperactivity Disorder and drugging children. While some parents may accept their child's diagnosis of ADHD, many are refusing the drugs altogether. Various advocacy groups are now filing law suits against drug companies for not listing adequately a wide range of side effects such as cardiovascular and central–nervous system problems known to accompany the use of Ritalin. The following story about one of my students exemplifies this:

Manuel at age eight was a normal, happy, active boy until the school pushed for him to go to the psychiatrists and medical establishment. He would not stay in his seat and pay attention, they said. He was subsequently diagnosed with ADHD, placed on Ritalin, and within three days was having petit mal seizures. This, according to his mother, is the reason that today Manuel has fine motor, gross motor, and learning problems. Manuel also spins when he walks down the hall and needs to change directions. "Not a lot can be done for his awkward movements," stated the local occupational and physical therapists that agreed to be "consultants". (See additional information on Manuel.)

For years as a teacher in the field of special education, I have seen a proliferation of referrals for ADHD when the emotionally impaired referral did not work. Well-meaning teachers perpetuate this, and, especially, psychologists who want an instant cure for some problem probably based on a communication break with the school or with learning in general. The psychologist, who, like the psychiatrist, rarely has a workable plan other than "Tell me about your day," wants that backup from the medical establishment. Then he has a fix and asks with great prestige, "Did you take your medication?" or suggests, "His medication probably needs to be adjusted." *The* plan in the final analysis is special education classes.

It is a hoax, a cruel one being played on our society and societies of the West. Our very future is at stake! These children are our future, and their future is at risk. I have observed these students rollercoaster from good to bad. I have seen these students off the drugs and on again. There are already indications that these drugs lead to addiction to other drugs. I have known a number of them who got into street drugs such as marijuana. What is the message that we are giving them? Take these drugs to calm yourself and make you concentrate better, but do not touch the drugs some of your classmates may be fooling around with on the side. The question we should ask the medical establishment is: 'What price are we paying for this temporary fix?' There have been stories in the news of elementary school–age children giving or selling their Ritalin to schoolmates. Have we seriously looked at what is really ailing our schools? Might there be answers within the schools once we identify the problem?

If we consider that we are spiritual beings, and few would doubt this, can we see that we are getting very far away from whom we really are. Today in education, we have become stimulus-response machines, and the spirit is no longer recognized as the life force within us. There is much evidence, gathered over thousands of years by all the great spiritual leaders of the past, which suggests that we are not machines. If we are drugged, then the spirit cannot exercise self-determinism over learning and acquisition of knowledge. Could

Learning Disabilities: The Myth

it be that we have not understood the problem? Might the problem be one that is inherent in study itself, and that the fast track is one of too much significance and too little application in today's schools? Might the problem be one of learning how to learn? Have we examined the barriers to study? Do students know their purpose for learning? Do they know what a student is? Can they define study? What are their misunderstood words on a subject? Are they taught to use the context to guess at a misunderstood word rather than define it and see that the word is fully understood? Is the study gradient too steep? Have they been given sufficient mass when they have not understood a word or concept? Do students know what they want to do with the subject matter they are studying? Can they apply it?

First the student needs to understand that help is available, to accept control and be willing to control his materials of study and himself. Next the student can generate some interest in his study when he becomes self-determined on it. He must be guided to an understanding of these concepts along with the most important one of all, communication. He can be taught application of material studied by learning communication skills that improve concentration for subjects, persons, or anything, and by addressing the three barriers to study: absence of mass, too steep of a study gradient, and the misunderstood word. Of course, the student does not necessarily make good progress across the board unless all teachers have been trained to recognize these barriers. Physiological symptoms accompany each of these barriers, leading to visits to the nurse, school absences, and more medication from doctors. For instance, there can be around twenty-six symptoms that accompany the misunderstood word, the most important of the barriers. I had a student come into my class the other day, holding her stomach. I asked, "Lara, what is wrong?" She replied, "My stomach is hurting, may I go to the nurse?" I said, "What class are you coming from?" She said, "Algebra." I asked, "Did you misunderstand anything?" She said, "Yes. We had this big problem that we worked on together on the board with the teacher, and I didn't get it."

Very often, teachers are themselves afflicted with misunderstood words in their own subject matter, and teaching, and education in general. Teachers work in a suppressive system that stresses coverage of the curriculum, so the gradient approach is thrown out automatically. There is little time for the addition of mass and checking for misunderstood words due to the significant amount of the subject that must be covered. A few years back, a colleague asked me what I meant by saying students need to use mass. I said, "What is the definition of mass?" He said, "Material." I said, "What does that mean?" Before he could give a complicated response, I held up the pen I was using and said, "It's this," and pointed to the desk, and various other objects. I said, "Remember, these objects, as well as films or pictures representing the real thing, are the mass the student needs. If these are not available, then something such as blocks or clay is necessary to help students demonstrate their understanding." He knew this, of course, but did not appear certain that he understood it. If he did, he would apply this in his teaching, and the students in his class would not be buried in all the significances of the subject he felt compelled to cover at lightening speed. Teachers trudge on believing that students' problems all stem from societal ills or last year's teacher. He said, "Nothing you're going to do is going to help this year's crop. They don't care about anything but sex, drugs and immediate pleasure." Eventually, teachers dig a hole for themselves and sink right where they are, along with their students. They sink because they do not have an answer to the problem of growing illiteracy in the classroom. But problems have solutions, and sometimes the answers are so simple that nobody wants to accept them. We tend to prefer information that sounds complex and comes from the infinite wisdom of those in the ivory towers of the universities. Thus, we are required to implement their "research findings" and ignore our observations and natural instincts, because it sounds wise. How dare we challenge the findings of the sages? When natural laws stare us in the face, how could a simple solution be true? A real solution must be complicated!

Recently, I had a conversation with the German mother of a fourteen-year-old boy who had been variously diagnosed as ADHD and dyslexic. He had been placed on Ritalin, but was fortunately taken off it by the mother, who sought help at a local clinic in Germany for dyslexic students. They told her that "hearing" (auditory) processing was the problem. She could ably quote all the terms that we use in

Learning Disabilities: The Myth

the field of special education for learning disabilities in the United States. What it boiled down to was that the boy needed to be on the proper gradient for learning to read, that this had been bypassed somehow. With the repetition given at a slower gradient, he is now reading, and with it comes the spelling and writing. He began clearing up his misunderstood symbols as he learned to decode. As a teacher of reading for students with reading deficits, I see this all the time. If the student has low average to average intelligence, he can learn to read unless there are severe to profound health problems or traumatic brain injuries. These students can learn, too, but the gradient would be lower and the rate slower

Drugs are not the answer, nor are they a way out of the nightmare in education. They are the way in and they are a cauldron that burns endlessly and stews the minds of our young people. Drugs are the problem along with the psychological and psychiatric solutions that have sunk us into the mire. Drugs cause us to sink only further into the abyss of misunderstood words, and prevent application. But there is hope and there is a way out. If we can address the student as a spiritual being who is drug-free and clear, we all win. If we give the students back to the teacher who is trained with the correct technology to do the job, we all survive. Take the self-determinism away from the student and the teacher, ply the student with drugs, and we all lose and spiral downward toward non-survival. We have the answer and we have the correct technology to do the job. Let's do it!

Sorting and Dividing

Thousands of students around the country are classified as Learning Disabled, Attention Deficit/Hyperactive or Emotionally Impaired and are enrolled in special education programs yearly, and the numbers are increasing at a mad rate. Too often children suspected of having ADHD or emotional problems are referred by schools for evaluations at local clinics, and then are labeled by the medical establishment. Generally, very little reliable data is given to warrant these labels and for the latter two, drugs are often prescribed.

In my system, most students are labeled as having a learning impairment based on processing or production of information that relates to an area of academic deficit. Frequently, they have short term or long-term memory retrieval problems. I have heard teachers over and over again say, 'He got it yesterday, but forgot it today'. The assessors would nod wisely in agreement, because this corroborated their findings. The student forgot it today because he never learned it in the first place. Had he been asked to apply and demonstrate his understanding, the teacher would have known that he had not understood the assignment. For certain, he did not understand the language of the individualized achievement tests and probably most of the questions he was asked that led to the label. He does not have a learning or memory problem nine times out of ten. He never understood most of what had been dished out in generous portions in his classes. He got hung up on something that he misunderstood a long time back. Therefore, he either became one who memorized but could not apply, or one who just sank into non-comprehension and utter failure. Both are at risk! They were never taught how to learn in the first place.

This sorting and dividing of students is disproportional when compared to what is considered the norm in our schools. We have all the different categories of students: Learning Disabled (mild - moderate), Learning Disabled (moderate – severe), EMR (educationally mentally retarded), EI (emotionally impaired), BD (behavior-disordered), ESL (English as second language), Slow Learners (slow rate), Gifted (above average to superior intelligence), AVID (college bound students, making Cs but ought to do better),

Learning Disabilities: The Myth

ADHD (Attention Deficit Hyperactivity Disorder), Dyslexic (reading disability), and no doubt some others. All these labels are handed out routinely in schools across the United States by teams of specialists trained in testing and labeling. With each of these groups comes a set of specific characteristics, reams of paperwork, accountability, and different ideas of what is the correct procedure to fix the problem and what is not. Psychologists and psychiatrists mix in this with their esoteric wisdom and non-workable solutions that even further confound teachers and parents on the receiving end.

All of these groups could be lumped together with all the students in the school. Then sort one time: those who take more time to learn and those who learn rapidly. The difference is the learning rate, not the amount of learning. All can learn and all can arrive. The student with learning disabilities cannot get things done. He has words he has misunderstood. Because information from his subjects was forced on him without his agreement, he cannot proceed. He cannot absorb all the data from his subjects, because he has lost the power of choice. He has become apathetic. By the time the student reaches high school, the parents have thrown in the towel and are grateful for anyone who can share the burden. They have been given a lot of the reasons why he is behaving as he is but never provided a workable plan. Most likely, the child has been placed on drugs or counseled behind closed doors. The wisdom from the child study teams is passed via the classroom teacher and specialists to the parent, but rarely does any of it help the child learn better. For example, the student who is identified as ADHD has to be made to work if he is to accomplish much. All these measures are temporary fixes and do nothing to decrease the learning lag.

How does all this sorting get started? I have a very good example handed to me by a good friend who just moved with his family from Germany to Spain. He is a principal at a school in Spain and has two children, both in elementary school. He wrote that he is very concerned about his youngest, a little boy about six years old in first grade. His wife, also a teacher, has been spending up to three exhausting hours a day after school working with their son. He describes the son's handwriting as "atrocious" but getting better. This is a very bright little boy, very gentle and kind, but rather shy.

My initial reaction was " Sounds like the study gradient is way too steep." I asked him if this was so. If the gradient is too steep I told him, it is doubtful that your son is going to catch up considering the misunderstood words that are coming his way. Because he is moving at a slower rate, he is going to need more time and, of course, the mass to handle his conceptual misunderstandings based on misunderstood words. He is going to need to clear up every single misunderstood word in his subjects. No doubt he has misunderstood symbols in his cursive writing; he needs practice and more practice but at a slower rate. If my estimation is correct, then his mother's work with him at the wrong gradient could lead to frustration for both of them. There is the chance that he is going to withdraw from learning, or become apathetic about it. This reaction may not be detectable at first. Before too long, if he is in an American school, the specialists are going to pounce on him and determine that "something is wrong with him" and decide that he is learning disabled. The specialists will decide that these learning problems stem from immaturity, developmental delay, ADHD, or any of the other myriad diagnoses. Giving the boy a label does not address the problem, only compounds it. The diagnosis and the overwhelming number of compiled misunderstood words and symbols could then lead him to a lack of self-determinism and control of his learning. Furthermore, it could even set up a learned helplessness when, in fact, there is nothing wrong but the gradient and rate.

With the new guidelines for diplomas versus certificates, it is imperative that all students have the opportunity to learn the same material. Yet, the experts have convinced the teachers that these students are never going to learn much, or cannot learn, or have this or that processing problem. Further, the experts say that nothing more can be expected from them, or that drugs can fix the problem so some data can be poured in. So how are the students labeled with learning disabilities going to survive? Our education system is suppressive and perpetuates this hierarchy of failure and frustrates students and teachers. It is based on a clutter of misunderstood words from the top down and the bottom up. We know that all students are not equal in their ability to quickly grasp and apply data. But they can learn. We as teachers sometimes are unclear on our purpose, our

Learning Disabilities: The Myth

roles, the student's role, and learning in general. But we can learn and improve our craft.

Given some power of choice over the data and placement on the correct study gradient, and clearing up misunderstood words, any student can learn. The difference for the student is in the learning rate, not the quantity of learning. Nor is the problem due to some *"processing"* problem. He can learn, but it is going to take more time and at a lower gradient. If we jump a gradient, he falls down, if the rate is too fast, he gets lost. If he has misunderstood words, he gets confused or presents other physiological symptoms. If we put the student on the correct gradient and proceed at the correct rate, he wins. But, if we cannot define what it is we are doing; *we* cannot proceed. And we all lose. Does the student know the purpose of the course we teach? Do we understand what we know?

Next, we need to have a look at what we are asking students to learn and how we are asking them to learn it. We have to decide what it is that we want students to know in a given subject. Not everything in each textbook is important, only important theories and reasons why the subject is being studied are. Important data *should* be memorized and application demonstrated. Mastery of the basics of any subject worth knowing should be learned thoroughly. Our curriculum is piled with significance, and teachers are in the business of filling students' heads with all this, putting in without requiring putting out. We want to force data in their heads, which were forced in ours. We produce glib students who cannot apply anything but make good marks, or we produce those who are utter failures. In between, there are some very clever students who learn and apply, but not many anymore. Just ask the business leaders in your communities or those in the universities, technical, and vocational schools.

The teacher has lost her confidence in observing a student and figuring out what that student's learning rate might be and slowly increasing it on a gradient scale, while she attends to the one who learns rapidly. In order to understand something, one must have a workable definition for it. If not, confusion clouds what one does. Most probably never bothered to define education, and even if one looked up the definition, a good one cannot be found. We go around talking about education, but do not know what it is. The head master at a private school in England told me recently that he got all the way to Oxford as a mathematics teacher and did not know the definition of math. Once he got the definition straightened out, he was able to proceed with his degree in mathematics.

Education means to apply that which is learned. Getting people to know something is useless; idiot savants know things, but they do not understand what they know, nor can they apply it. So you have to understand what you know. Some pieces of information need to be committed to memory, reasons why need to be learned about a particular subject, but there are not that many facts of major importance in each textbook. What is important is that the student learns to apply the information that *is* important, that he be taught on a gradient scale, clarify all misunderstood words, and use mass to build and reinforce concepts. The student needs the opportunity to observe and figure out things based on these observations. He needs to create something that he can use. There is quite an excellent teacher in the science department at my school who has students invent something to know. The only problem is that the rate is too fast and the gradient is often too steep for most of the students on the lower-achievement end in her class. And she has to contend with the student who has learned the wrong lessons.

Eliminate these specialized groupings of students identified, modified, and passed along. Very few have learned much unless they were fortunate enough to have had some good vocational programs that required a lot of application. The student who cannot apply has no self-determinism on the data and has not understood it, because it is enforced and, therefore, not taken seriously. Students I have taught know a lot of things; they have learned a lot of wrong lessons and are fixated on these wrong lessons. They know little that they can apply in today's society to survive well. The student with the "Learned Helplessness Syndrome," the one I call "Mommy Do It," is a good example. He has been told for so long that something is wrong with him that he has become apathetic about learning, so you had just better do it for him. He has learned the lesson that his mommy would fix it, and later on in school, it is the teacher's turn. Now it is quite a challenge to undo this wrong lesson and get him

Learning Disabilities: The Myth

self-determined. This is an aberration and bars the door to learning and application.

Each year or so the education system revises the law, reauthorizes it or develops a new slant on the old one. This year the President and his education advisors are saying, "No child left behind." It sounds humane and wise! It is as if we can chant this and, magically, no child will be left behind. This creates a frantic effort to get more students into special programs so they can have an IEP that allows them to graduate. These lawmakers and politicians have always been able to say and write what was politically right but could never have implemented anything themselves. Why? Because they have a major misconception of learning and education and never conceived of a workable plan.

Most politicians answer the education dilemma by putting more money into the education system. For instance, my school system, which is worldwide, has been allocated $56.5 million for special education alone to be dispersed over the next six years beginning in 2003. Districts are spending it at a rapid rate on computer software, in-focus machines, training for computerized reading programs, and training on everything they can fund in hopes of improving learning. But no one ever asked me, or any of the hundreds of other teachers, what would help to improve learning. Yet, we are required to implement programs and use software handed down as the gospel. The decision makers go into a frenzy to get the money spent, all well meaning in most cases, but rarely does it trickle down to make a better student. Thus far, I have seen little that reduces my paperwork, meetings, and related duties so that I can spend more time planning *and* teaching. As a matter of fact, the maximum number of students that each special education teacher can now have on an individual caseload has increased. At the same time, aide hours have been increased to the same as teacher hours, but there is no money for aide substitutes. How does increasing aide hours beyond the school day benefit the program? With all the money that we are pouring into schools, we should be doing a better job. But we are not.

The special education law, Public Law 94-142, now IDEA (Individuals with Disabilities Education Act, recently reauthorized in 2004), mandated that students be taken out of the mainstream in the beginning, then they insisted that students be put back in the regular classes with "proper" modifications. With the rigor of the curriculum at my school, the students are being pulled back out again for math and English. At the same time, students in many states are now required to pass exit exams in order to earn a diploma; otherwise, they earn certificates. This leads more and more teachers to teach to the exam. There is a workable plan, and most teachers know how to go about teaching, but rarely have they been asked, and so their ideas were ignored

An overview of Hubbard's Study Technology shows how all of these groups could learn independently on checksheets. A checksheet is a form which sets out the exact sequence of items to be studied or done, in order, item by item on a course. It lists all the materials of the course in order to be studied with a place for the student to put his initial and the date as each item on the checksheet is studied, performed or checked out. The checksheet is the program that the student follows to complete that course. (This definition is from the Applied Scholastics course booklet: "How to Write a Checksheet" based on the works of L. Ron Hubbard.) Each student proceeds at his own gradient until he passes each part with 100-percent mastery. The technology requires precision in delivery. Therefore, a teacher would be trained in this method of study technology and could give the student a checkout on each section as required. In the beginning an assistant, not necessarily college-trained, would be preferable to assist in a regular-size class. This assistant should be trained precisely as an instructor in using Study Technology. As students grasp the technology, they become more and more self-sufficient and are then able to assist their peers and become self-learners. Students at different levels, and even on different courses, could progress at their own rate of learning in a single classroom.

Study Technology works! The student would demonstrate with clay, or use a demonstration kit with different colored blocks of various sizes, or sketches to show understanding of data. The student is checked on the understanding of randomly selected words. Certain data must be committed to memory and checked by the instructor or student's partner. If the student fails any part, he must go back and restudy until he has achieved mastery. A written exam is given at the end of a lesson or course and must be passed with 100-percent mastery. Again, if he misses anything, he must restudy and retest. This continues throughout all the basics of each of the courses. Then the students will be ready for courses where there are lectures and discussions on a steeper gradient. Although this may sound arduous, it really is not. In fact, students begin to delight and take pride in every single step that is mastered and checked off. They realize that they are making progress and each little step is a step up the bridge of learning. They are in charge of their school life and can achieve something that no one can take away from them.

We must observe our students and identify what the problem really is in our schools. At the same time, we should search out the best technologies being used around the globe that are producing bright and able students who can apply what they have learned. We need to see how *they* learned and find out if there is a pattern of producing achievement and learning. Study Technology has already been introduced to over 70 countries at the last count. Ministers of Education have welcomed Study Technology with open arms and requested its implementation in their countries, once they have experienced the amazing results from its application. Individual teachers in various public schools and universities throughout the United States have begun to use this technology in their teaching, and students are making huge gains like never before. Currently, studies are being conducted in a rural school district in Mississippi, where the teachers, desperate for help to stem the dropout rate caused by failure, are also reaching for Study Technology. There are a number of good models for us to follow like Greenfields School in England and the Delphi Schools in the United States who use Study Technology.

In this era of teacher shortage, fewer teachers would be required for overhauling a system that is already burdened with specialists and non-productive consultants. A workable plan would end the sorting and dividing of students. Students would learn and could apply what they learned. The specialist syndrome would come to a halt. These specialists could join the ranks of the regular classroom teachers. All would be trained on a gradient to apply this technology. Only one course is required to start! Teachers would be free to teach.

The student either knows and can apply the data, or he does not. If he does, he continues on the gradient; if he does not, he goes back over it until mastery is achieved. Given that these students all have low average to average intelligence, they can do it, just at a different learning rate. I have never had a student in special education that could not learn where the learning rate was considered and the student was placed on the correct study gradient. The problem exists when he enters the content classes where the gradient is very steep; he is overwhelmed with misunderstood words and concepts. This takes away his self-determinism and causes the special education teachers to implement IDEA and demand all kinds of modifications. Falling back on the special education guidance usually gets the student through the course with maybe a C, and, eventually, he will get a diploma. But does this diploma certify that he can apply anything that he has "learned"? Is a diploma what we want? Or do we want a graduate who has certainty on what he knows and can apply?

The same consideration goes for the other specialized groups. For example, the ESL (English as a Second Language) students must learn English first! Until they learn the fundamentals of English, they cannot proceed if they are being taught in English. This is also taught on a gradient of learning. We currently have a student at our high school who came to us three years ago from Ghana with no English whatsoever. If she had one or two words, she never used them. She did have an ESL teacher who worked very hard with her one period per day in a one-on-one situation. I suggested that she be placed in my very basic reading class, which was still too steep of a gradient, so I cut back and slowed the rate. This worked. These two classes were the only beneficial ones for her until she learned English. Her progress was slow, and it was not enough to handle the overwhelming amount of data handed out in the other courses. She did not understand English because the gradient had been way too steep for all her classes. There she sat in geometry lab, fiddling at the computer program and pretending to do something. This year, she has begun to stay home rather than face the day with all the non-comprehension. It is rather remarkable that she comes at all. She needs to be taught English first! Meanwhile, some in the school want a graduation plan for her, never mind if she learns anything. So the *experts* were contacted and asked to place her in special education, if a way could be found. The notion was that she appeared retarded! She was not retarded and not a Slow Learner; she did not *know* English!

We could put this study technology in our schools with no extra cost; in fact, in the long run we would save millions of dollars by ending the bulk of the specialist jobs that exist in the mild to moderate learning disabilities programs. (I am not talking about students with severe problems that require specialized help in the areas of physical therapy, occupational therapy and speech. But these services could also be streamlined.) Students would be individualized because they are working on a gradient scale and progressing at their own rate. The learning curve would go up, the desired statistic would go up – students demonstrating mastery and application of course content – or the desired statistic would go down – fewer students in special classes, fewer dropouts. There would be less teacher, parent, and student stress overall. Students would know that they could graduate and apply what they had learned. There would be no sorting and dividing, because it would not be necessary. No one would have to be told that something was wrong with him. He would have a certainty on the data that he had learned and at the same time be self-determined. This is the true type of individualization that we need, a system for *all* based on learning rate and that addresses the three barriers to study with the specific remedies. This would be the way to turn our schools around, leaving *no* child behind, save money, and save our future!

Marta L Marchisan, Ph D

IQ Can Be Raised

According to *Second College Edition: The American Heritage Dictionary,* (c. 1991, Houghton Mifflin Co.), intelligence is the capacity to acquire and apply knowledge. This is the definition that I follow when I look over my students and set a program for them. Will the student be able to solve the problems he is going to face in life? Will he be able to survive well at school, with his family, and on a job? Can he use all his perceptions in an efficient manner to apply the acquired knowledge? The field of psychology, on the other hand, sorts people based on intelligence scores ($\pm$ the standard deviation, of course), places them on the bell-shaped curve, and indicates that this score is fixed for life with little chance for improvement. These intelligence scores on assessment reports then tend to prejudice those who are required to make plans for students identified for help. Right at the outset, we limit ourselves, not to mention the student's future in education, by this wrong thinking.

As I began to examine the testing data of students transferring from different states into my special education program, I found broad discrepancies from one examiner to another and differing admission criteria and labeling practices from state to state. All agreed that they were following the law, but nothing was standardized. A student could have a bona fide learning disability in one state and no disability whatsoever in another system. Then the student had to be tested if tests were not current in order to qualify for the current program. More unnecessary work and time away from teaching this student. These records provided little or no useful information for instruction.

This brings to mind a student, Lynnette, who entered my program three years ago as a tenth-grader. She had been identified for the first time a month before she was to be transferred overseas to her new school in Germany. The records showed that she was intellectually deficient, with borderline retardation and adaptive behavior deficits. This struck me as odd anyhow that a student suddenly would be identified so very late in her academic career, end of ninth grade, as intellectually deficient. Such a student should have surfaced years ago and been placed in a special education program, especially with

Learning Disabilities: The Myth

adaptive deficits. It could happen that she was missed, but not this student. Within a few days, it was clear that Lynnette had behavior problems and high resistance to doing anything in the classroom. She suffered from lack of control at home. Her intelligence appeared normal, though at the low end. It was not long before she was a social butterfly and spent all her time talking and engaging in non-productive tasks in her classes.

During the initial parent interview, her mother had said that a private evaluator (psychologist) outside the school had stated that she was the worst case of ADHD he had ever seen. Now how did he know that? See, the school had doubted that she was intellectually deficient and was shilly-shallying about placement. This prompted the mother to go outside the school for an evaluation. Nearly every time, a label of ADHD will be placed on such a student, if all else fails, in order to get a homework supervisor. This provided a clue to me that the school was probably a bit intimidated by the parent's demand that something be done about her daughter's failing grades, and thought it safer to find something wrong with her. I saw no symptoms of classic ADHD in either of the classes she had with me, Reading and Learning Strategies. Nor had any of the teachers reported inattentiveness. They did report that she would not do her work, talked constantly, and did not accept responsibility for her work. As a matter of fact, she was extremely attentive and well behaved within the tight boundaries of my class. Reading comprehension was low, but math was not extremely deficient. As time went by, she began to act up more and more in her regular academic classes, socializing, sassing teachers, and not completing work. One teacher was very frustrated with Lynnette and reported that she was sitting on the floor in a dress with her legs spread eagle to the delight of some male students. I said, "Tell her to get up immediately and sit in a chair!" Simple, right? But some teachers lose their own self-determinism about how to correct the obvious. They have been brainwashed that the specialists are the only ones who can solve the problems.

It appeared that she was a full-blown behavior problem, who had not understood her purpose as a student and was not motivated to learn. She was not motivated to learn because she had not been taught *how* to learn. This is *the* missing ingredient in our teaching methodologies. I was able to straighten out the behavior in my classes fairly quickly by establishing good control. The problem was that the control did not carry over to other classes. The only alternative was to provide her an escort and have someone sit beside her in class to see that she did her work. Police work, as I call it, rarely works, and it is a huge waste of resources, but we are authorized to do it in special education. The work could be completed but it did not allow her self-determinism, and therefore, this work ethic would not generalize or stick without the stimulus of my aide or me. She needed to become self-determined about her own learning, and this would not happen immediately but on a gradient.

One day, she was requested to report to me during seminar to do some make-up work and get extra help. I waited, and she did not show up. (I was allowing her to be self-determined, I thought.) When my aide located her, she was in the music room unsupervised and braiding another student's hair and refused to come. She told my aide, "I'm busy." I went to fetch her; when I found her, she was still braiding another student's hair. I said, "Lynnette, come with me." She continued braiding the hair and without looking up said, "I'm busy!" That did it! I replied very forcefully and with full intention, "You come with me *now*!" She was furious, but did as I requested and followed me to my room. There were consequences after we defined responsibility. That was the only problem I ever had with her, but she could raise Cain in any number of classes and get into fights in the hallway at the drop of a hat.

The next year, she was evaluated and did not qualify for the program. She had progressed and was passing her other classes, and the intelligence test showed that she was within the low average range. The adaptive behavior analysis showed that she was functioning as any normal student her age should. This was quite an increase from the intellectually deficient range; it also disqualified her from my program because she did not meet the other criteria. Of course, a lot of factors could have contributed to this leap in her score: errors in the previous psychological testing, increase in motivation and responsibility due to good control, an understanding of help, better communication and self-determinism kicking in.

Learning Disabilities: The Myth

What she had that lowered her intelligence score, I am convinced, were a lot of misunderstood words in reading that impacted her comprehension of just about everything. Putting her under hydraulic press, so to speak, with good control and teaching her how to study raised her intelligence score considerably. It also wiped out any doubt that she was or could have been retarded. This was the trend then that I noted: reading problems and key words that were never defined and understood in her various subjects. These undefined words had become a stumbling block to any further gain in a particular subject. The gradient approach to reading and vocabulary development helped her make considerable gains. At one point, she had the highest grade on a research and writing project in U.S. history, done entirely on her own.

Lamar was a challenge because of his academic history and behaviors. He looked as if he might have suffered from a birth injury causing retardation with his overweight and odd shaped body, and oversized ears. He rarely shut his mouth; it hung open as if the hinge in his jaws was sprung. Yet, his behaviors in class were those of the typical ADHD student; he thumped, doodled, and was in and out of his seat. In reality, his symptoms were related to a whole heap of misunderstood words. Lamar was spoiled to the nth degree by his parents, especially his mother, who made excuses for everything he did. Although she had accepted him as retarded, she clung to the hope that he could be fixed. I accepted excuses for nothing and accepted him as having nothing wrong with him. This worked! It worked so well that it worked wonders!

Lamar had always been educated with retarded students. When he arrived in my classroom, the first major challenge was getting him to stay in his seat and stop the thumping, doodling, and other non-productive behaviors. This was done by establishing good control and defining the boundaries, with consequences for overstepping them. As I adjusted the gradient of the curriculum for him, provided some mass, and had him clear up definitions of words at his reading grade level, he began to improve. He improved so much that he was doing introductory algebra independently, and doing well. Although he needed a lot of help with world history his second year with me, it became his favorite class. His reading grade level was extremely low, though improving weekly. I discovered that he had the ability to listen very well when he understood what was going on in the classroom. This ability helped him learn in all his classes. He began to work tirelessly to complete his world history assignments and study with me for his tests. As his grades improved, his confidence soared.

Although he did test my limits on occasion, generally, he progressed. I used humor to push him along when he became lazy. One day his first year with me, I sent him down to his world regions teacher with his project that he had just thrown together and told him to tell his teacher, 'Here's my project that I just slapped together last period!' He actually repeated what I'd told him. Anyhow, it was hilarious to his teacher, who did not penalize him at all. He became more responsible and began to catch on to me during his second year, especially when I promised to find him a good wife. At our school, all students are invited to participate in a data match once a year, a project for one of the business classes, and Lamar asked me to help him put down his specifications for his dream woman. I did. That was the last time he allowed me to do that. Besides, he found a girlfriend without my assistance. Also, he discovered that girls liked jewelry, flowers and pretty things, so he got a job bagging groceries to support her needs. (Guess I failed; I'd planned to get him a wife that would support him!)

By the end of the third year, his reading had improved tremendously and he was becoming more independent, and amazingly did not even look retarded anymore. His physical appearance changed dramatically just by the way he carried himself and spoke. He had confidence that he could *do* something. When testing time rolled around, guess what? His IQ was within the low-average range. Come marking time, his mother was proud as a peacock as she strutted about with his report card, talking to teachers and accepting congratulatory messages as if the effort were totally hers, and glad that she had produced such a son. Lamar thought he was a Rhodes Scholar! He had gotten some reality on learning along with a good dose of self-determinism.

There are numerous such stories; the important thing is that the underlying theme of each student is the same, ruling out those with genetic defects and traumatic brain injuries. All have misunderstood words in various subjects that were never addressed; all have reading deficits. Students can learn to read and can define and understand the words they read, write, and speak. Students must be taught to observe and use all their perceptions. Students must drill *and* drill what they have learned until they can apply it flawlessly. Students must be given the power of choice to apply this knowledge in meaningful work. With this increase in understanding and application, students become competent, and intelligence quotients rise. Students can rise to greater heights in literacy and understand their school subjects. No doubt about it!

On Behavior

Special education has become the dumping ground for students with conduct disorders. Time and again these students who refuse to do class work or homework are diagnosed very quickly by a clinical psychologist or psychiatrist as having Attention Deficit Hyperactive Disorder and placed on Ritalin or some other drug to help them focus. Parents are all too willing to accept this diagnosis in the hope that someone else can share in the role of getting this student to do his work and progress in school. Although there is growing debate about the efficacy of placing such children on drugs, some parents see taking drugs as the lesser of the evils, while others refuse medication but insist upon having their child labeled and placed in special education. With the help of psychiatrists and the medical profession, these students *will* find themselves on the roles of special education. They *will* be categorized ADHD (Attention Deficit/Hyperactivity Disorder) or ADHD with LD (Learning Disability characteristics) or EI (Emotionally Impaired), because their behavior was not managed.

What I have observed over and over are students with reading problems accompanied by behavior problems. Both these problems can be managed with good control and by understanding the three barriers to study. Placing the student on the proper study gradient, instructing him how to define his misunderstood words and clear them in a good dictionary to full conceptual understanding, and providing him with mass for application, will correct any problem in learning. This is the magic that is at our fingertips as teachers and parents. A precise method of learning how to learn can fix the problem.

The typical ADHD student has mild learning problems, if at all, but for a multitude of reasons will not do his homework. He has lost interest and self-determinism. Teachers report, "They can do the work, if they would. They are just disorganized and off-task." They thump, doodle, look off into the distance, are in and out of their seats, and are not in present time. Parents say the same thing. Not too long ago, a Latino mother made a surprise visit to my classroom after school to check on her son who was doing make-up work in Algebra I. She came down on him like a hornet when I told her

Learning Disabilities: The Myth

he was not bothering to do his algebra homework and would not complete his work in class. She got right in his face and said, "I am going to beat you for every problem that you did not do, and then I am going to slap you for every one you did not finish!" I rather enjoyed this scene and had to bite my tongue to keep from howling. It was hilarious watching her face getting red and blending into her fiery, curly, red hair teased to the max. Hands on her hips, her eyes strained in their sockets as she berated her son. Although I knew that she was only bluffing, and the boy knew it, too, it did me a world of good anyway to experience this vivid demonstration on a Friday afternoon after a long, hard week. The boy had lost all self-determinism about learning a long time ago, giving over his responsibility to his mother, and became rather apathetic about learning in general. He had been diagnosed with ADHD, but the mother had had enough wisdom to take him off the drugs soon after he started.

A student presenting the so-called ADHD symptoms could be a student who is suffering from allergies or a host of other things that interfere with concentration. He could also have a present-time problem, or someone in his family or school has suppressed him. Many of these students suffer from lack of self-determinism, lack of good control and always misunderstand key words in their subjects that were never clarified.

Although very few have severe reading problems, their misunderstood words tend to pile up, and this lends itself to reading deficiencies and can cause the student to exhibit physiological and mental symptoms when he comes across a word that he does not understand. One symptom described in L. Ron Hubbard's *Basic Study Manual* is that the student can go blank right after a misunderstood word. He gets hung up here and cannot concentrate on anything else. These are all contributing factors to aberration in the classroom. Generally, these so-called ADHD students are not the products of special education, unless it is secondary to a severe learning problem, but these students fill the roles under bogus diagnoses. And rarely is a plan set up for them by the well-meaning medical establishment. The recommendation is take the medicine, and this will handle the problem. The end result, though, is a zombie who is much worse off than before and still has not learned responsibility for himself or his learning. He is at risk for a whole lot of other side effects, not to mention street drugs.

Many, many students that have come through the doors of my classroom have been on one drug or another. Most were placed on drugs by psychiatrists for ADHD, the most popular, followed by depression. A student that qualified recently as learning impaired is in the ninth grade and has a host of problems due to Ritalin. Manuel is a new student for me this year, likeable, friendly, and tries to do his work when supervised. He has a range of problems from organization to math and reading deficits. He cannot remember things and is described as forgetful by his teachers. Our local clinic wanted to be consultants only for physical therapy and occupational therapy until the teachers and I ganged up on them. Immediately, I placed Manuel on a plan to rehabilitate the learning, organization, and communication with the gradient approach and good control.

His mother, rightfully, refused further evaluation by the psychiatrist and medical team because she feared another round of drugs. Actually, he would not have then qualified for special education because there were no processing deficits (criteria in this system for learning disability status), and Other Health Impaired status requires a medical doctor's decision. See the game? We qualified him anyway under learning disabled as a professional decision. This was stretching it; however, he was the most needy student I had all last year. By the end of first quarter of this year, Manuel was making great gains in Algebra I and "Killing the algebra tutor," according to his algebra teacher. This was a huge leap and improvement from his labored struggle and slow gradient of Introduction to Algebra. It was a step-by-step approach, defining every misunderstood word. Of course, the amount of homework was decreased considerably due to his motor problems.

I worked on organization with Manuel by having him do a shakedown of his backpack every day. He enters my room looking like Santa Claus with his backpack crammed to the brim; he can never find a thing. Another strategy I used was to get a set of text books sent home, so that he would not have to carry them around with him, and it would be easier on his back. Still, there was loose

Learning Disabilities: The Myth

paper everywhere. Eventually, he got his materials and papers under control, organized and into color-coded binders. Until now, he had accepted no responsibility for his learning and had no hope, I think, of ever doing much better. Now he is confronting his problem head-on and doing something about it.

At his previous school, he had been placed in a class for retarded students. I realized that he was mimicking the behavior of students who had not all been taught adaptive and social skills of dining properly. Manuel came to my class every day right after lunch with spaghetti sauce smeared all over his face, or whatever was on that day's menu. I spoke to him privately and suggested that his appearance was part of my environment and the environment of others and that he had a responsibility here to look presentable. Perhaps, he had not noticed or confronted this before. I told him to go have a good look in the mirror in my room. He did. With one more reminder, the problem cleared up.

Sasha came to me with Tourette's syndrome and a long history of special education. In fact, she had been in special education all her life, had been home-schooled for the last three years and was now on drugs for the Tourette's. At the most inopportune times, she would burst forth with a loud hiccough that, a few decibels higher, could shatter the panes in the windows. She had never had a regular reading class, although she loved to read. In Sasha's records, her former teacher had declared, "She reads on about a fourth-grade level, but her silent reading is about a twelfth-grade level." Now what in the world did she mean by that? I discovered that Sasha had invented definitions of many of the words she read or would bypass misunderstood words altogether, using context cues to guess at the meaning. Right away, I assigned her to my reading and English class and a learning strategies class to support her other academic classes.

Slowly she progressed to where the syndrome disappeared when she demanded that she be taken off the medicine her final year in high school. She said, "The drug changed my personality and made me want to sleep all the time. Also, it has caused me to gain weight." She was taken off the drug, and her Tourette's never returned for the remainder of the year. She had confronted whom she was, the so-called Tourette's, and could now proceed. Sasha had learned all about communication and its importance in succeeding in life. Slowly, she was able to understand the suppression she experienced at home with her father and was better able to communicate with him. Eventually, she discovered that she could handle suppression at home and in her life. By looking at it and understanding it, suppression no longer had an effect on her. She was not stressed by it, and her somatics, the tic that was diagnosed as Tourette's syndrome, disappeared along with the suppression.

Sasha used to capture every spare fifteen minutes I could give her; she talked and I listened. I would illustrate situations with colored blocks to provide her a model for understanding. Soon, she was manipulating the blocks, or sketching to describe her communication problems. Of course, we defined communication and problem. She found out that her emotions were okay and that she could feel any emotion she wanted. She just needed to show the right emotion for the right situation; anything else would not be appropriate. This could bring her down. She even began to modulate her voice and lower the volume. Her loudness had been a source of irritation to other students and me because she always sounded hostile.

By the end of her third and final year, she had gained sufficient confidence in her ability to succeed. With the knowledge of word clarification, reading, and some communication training, Sasha blossomed into one of the best students in regular English her senior year. That's right, she no longer needed a special reading class. She could read and understand Macbeth with the best of them. She had maintained herself on the honor roll every year, and her psychosomatics had disappeared along with very questionable learning problems. For sure, she had had reading deficits that had been severe, but with the gradient approach, clarifying misunderstood words, and using mass as needed, she had evolved from a girl with a history of invalidation that had nearly flattened her spirit into a responsible and able young woman. At graduation she received the Presidential Award signed by President Bush, for considerable achievement and overcoming insurmountable obstacles.

At the beginning of the school year, I was called by the new principal to talk to one of the students in special education who had

Learning Disabilities: The Myth

gotten himself into trouble. He had had an altercation with a female student in his first-period computer class. He was swearing and threatening the girl, gave her a push, and drew his fist back to strike when the teacher ordered him to the office. Radam at seventeen had a history of assault and battery, juvenile detention, and jail as he called it, plus failing grades and little academic progress before coming to our school. Here was a being who had nearly given up on the American system of education, for it had not helped him.

Radam had seen failure over and over again, and experienced punishment for his violent temper. He displayed these charged outbursts because he had lost his dignity and sunk into apathy about learning. Radam was apathetic about learning because he was required to spend time in classes where there was very little that he understood. His skills were dismally low, especially in the area of reading comprehension. He was streetwise and belonged to a gang that he quickly established upon arrival at our school. Radam had been in my reading class for a short time, but was removed and placed in a computer reading program. One day he asked, "Why did you take me out of your reading class?" I replied, "Why do you ask?" He said, "I was *learning* something." The reading had been on a very low, slow gradient, clearing up every single misunderstood word or symbol. I recall one day, he had gone to the board and was asked to write a lower-case cursive letter f. He could not, nor could he write or read a lot of cursive letters. So the gradient approach had worked, but it was too late for Radam in my class. I knew that Radam needed a different type of reading at this stage, one that would address key words in his job.

Before I could engineer a reading plan for him, his mother had snatched him out of school and secretly whisked him away to a drug rehabilitation program. It was right about the time of a local bank heist, and I had the strong suspicion that he had been involved, but he was not. Instead, he was being treated for depression, following a drying-out program, and was under psychiatric care. Then he was placed on psychotropic drugs to help him manage his "bipolar depression." Swap one drug for another. Does that make sense? When Radam returned, he was never the same. He was filled with even more anger and resentment and displayed frequent fiery outbursts of temper. Yes, he returned to his gang and peddling street drugs. This was his haven, the only place where he felt some measure of respect. Although I had not objected to his removal from my reading program because of his volatile behavior, I was concerned about what the future held for him. Already he had made extreme threats of violence against a younger female student in my class who was annoying enough to make a preacher cuss. At the time, I told my former principal, "Radam is a time bomb ready to explode! We have to do something. The program is not right for him."

When I entered her office, the principal asked, "What do I do next?" I said, "Let me speak to him first." I would speak to the teacher later. I interviewed Radam for his description of the incident and made notes. When I had the statement of the teacher, which agreed with Radam's, he signed it. All the while during the interview, he was looking at me directly. Eventually, the teacher walked in and sat down. He is a very capable, low-key individual, but firm with discipline. He began talking to Radam in a low voice, explaining that he was never going to win in a situation with a female, no matter if the female was wrong. I noticed that Radam suddenly became defensive, turned to the side, and would not look at him. Why? Because he was evaluating for Radam. Radam had already agreed with me that he knew the difference between right and wrong.

His mother and stepfather had had their phone shut off for not paying their bill, and, as a result, they could not be reached. Radam said he could not be placed in the small room beside the principal's office because he had already been in "jail" (juvenile detention). Instead, he was placed in a larger room and requested some paper and a pen along with a book. I brought him these items, then talked to him about writing as therapy. I told how I had kept a journal for about a year and that I had worked out some problems this way. More importantly, I drew a diagram of a body with a circle around the head and explained with a dot in the center of the circle that he was a spirit, that it was not the color of his skin, his achievement level, or failing grades that made him who he was, but it was his spirit. I explained that as a spirit, he had infinite potential. For a brief moment, his eyes were bright and shining, and he sighed, a release of the pent-up charge that he had held inside all morning while he was being re-stimulated in the classroom by previous failures.

One of the first questions one of the counselors put to me later on in the week in a meeting was, "Is Radam taking his medication?" That comment and reminder almost made me sick. He had been placed on psychotropic drugs that would only develop a dependency but not address the problem. What would be our plan to help him learn? As it turned out, there was not enough time or trained staff to help Radam correct his problem.

Within weeks, he was expelled for possession of marijuana and assaulting one of the faculty members. He slugged the teacher in the jaw, dangerously close to the eye, in front of at least five witnesses and while talking to his mother on the phone. I was one of the witnesses, and I asked the father and police to bring him to my room so they could sort things out. Radam looked like an animal; his rage and anger had gone, and he sank way, way down on the scale of human emotions. He knew his school life here was finished. I would not have recognized him if someone had taken a photo at that instant and later requested me to identify him. I spoke to him softly and saw tears on his cheeks, probably the first he had ever shed in public. Shortly, the police took him away, but not before they frisked him at the front door of the school in full public view with his arms stretched above his head and legs spread apart. I will never forget the scene as they placed Radam's hands behind him, locked them in handcuffs, and led him to the patrol car. I had a lump in my throat that burned and prevented me from swallowing as I stood by and watched, helpless. We in education and society had failed this boy. Where was *my* responsibility in all this?

These students, with no agreement on learning and, therefore, no self-determinism, can follow a life of crime. They have lost their dignity. Without exception, they have huge numbers of misunderstood words and symbols and reading problems. They do not know their purpose, do not understand what study is, and do not know how to learn. They look for something within a group, a symbol of power, a temporary respite from their inner turmoil. They eventually start the downward spiral toward self-destruction. These students become a burden to themselves, not to mention society. Many wind up in jails and become repeat offenders, if they survive. Why? Our education system is not set up to deal with them. We deal with them through force and exclusion when they begin to commit crimes against the environment. Force, because we offered them help and they refused it. But was it help? Could they receive it? Did they understand the flows of help? Were they taught how to learn?

There is a way to salvage these students before it is too late. It is very simple to place them on a gradient of learning and clear up every single misunderstood word and concept. They must be supplied the mass and demonstrate their understanding. At the same time, the amount of text must be reduced, and application of the learning must be shown. However, the entire school must agree to such a plan for the gradient approach and technology to work. Ethics and communication skills must be taught and reinforced daily. An ethics office with highly trained persons could handle each behavior incident and provide a workable plan. A course in communication would be required for all, including teachers and staff. If a system like this were in place, we would not need to seek the help of the local military police to control the students during unstructured time at my school. What message are we sending our students? Are we saying that something outside the student causes him to behave the way he does? Are we telling him that he, a spiritual being, cannot control his behavior? We can no longer depend on the home to provide this training. They, too, are products of education systems that lacked the technology to handle today's overwhelming changes and demands on students. Therefore, we must take on this responsibility. The choice is ours: we pay now, or we pay later.

I have witnessed the diagnosis for emotionally impaired for students with all types of problems since I have been teaching, but I have never seen an insane student in the regular classroom. Yet, I have seen and worked with some very severe students in private centers before becoming a teacher. What I have seen in public schools are students who are acting-out due to lack of control or who are suffering from suppressive persons (the truly insane ones) in their midst, or any combination of these. I have also seen students who have been misdiagnosed in order to receive services and get some help with their homework. The majority of the diagnoses have been

Learning Disabilities: The Myth

for depression or a variation of that, and a prescription for drugs is usually given.

I had one such student, Mike, who was a con artist at report card time. He would become despondent suddenly, and his mother would haul him over to the local clinical psychologist, who would ask, "Is he taking his medication?" or "Perhaps his medication needs to be changed." His brother and sister were on the honor roll, and Mike had slacked off all quarter and now had to face the music. He was depressed said the psychologist. Had the psychologist investigated, he would have found that Mike had been in high spirits most of the quarter, into devilment, tearing up the science lab, and setting off stink bombs, never completing work independently. He was a criminal in the making. He was not emotionally disturbed but rather a student who had some reality break on learning a long time ago and never could read at grade level. Mike was very sharp, but just not interested in schooling. He had learned the wrong lessons of lying, stealing, and avoidance of work, which got attention from those around him for his antics and disruptive behavior. Good control worked in my classroom, but it never transferred to other classes. One day I timed him to see how long it would take for him to grasp the information in a study guide for world history. It took him eight minutes, and he knew it cold. I would not call this emotionally impaired, ADHD, or learning impaired, though he had carried these various diagnoses at one time or another. His mother, I might add, treated him as a best friend rather than son. So control was out. He had had a history of bad control or even no control.

Someone has invalidated these students, and the drugs never help but only create a dependency, alter the student's personality, and cause general suffering. These students do need help for sure, but drugs are not the answer. Drugs should be used only in the most extreme cases to save a life. Unfortunately, I have never seen a plan beyond the drugs. Oh, the clinical psychologist may recommend counseling for the family or student. Mostly, these clinics deal with evaluating the student and making recommendations already in place. Nothing new is offered: referral to special education and a prescription for drugs.

Jackie could not get herself to school no matter the cajoling and encouragement of the teaching staff. This was a problem of long duration, and by the end of the second quarter of her first year in high school, she had piled up forty absences. Why? It was a dangerous environment. Why? She was afraid to make a mistake. I began slowly with Jackie on a low gradient of, "Hello, glad to see you today" or "How are you?" Sometimes, "Do you need any help?" At first her attendance did not improve, but her comfort level in my classroom did. She began talking to the other females in the small seminar class that I held and was building some friendships. She was accepted and even began to read history together with another student. I noted that her reading was not smooth and apparently there were misunderstood words.

In this class was another student whom I had taught for three years and was now coming to me for guidance about personal issues. Generally, I take students with personal problems over to my office so that they can speak in private. Sasha did not care if we talked at my desk, and she was perfectly willing to share her secrets with all if they were interested. I use blocks and diagrams when students discuss personal issues with me and never evaluate for them. Basically, I listen. It is marvelous because the student solves her own problem. Well, Jackie overheard some of these conversations and began to edge over to me during the next few classes.

Finally, one afternoon, Jackie sat and talked—nothing extremely private—about her life with her grandmother before she came to Germany. The next day, I received a fiery e-mail from her mother, who by now had worn out her welcome with Jackie's teachers and both administrators with her suppressive communications, telling me to leave the counseling up to the counseling department. What did the psychologist do when he did see Jackie? He asked, "How was your day?" according to her own report. Did that translate to school attendance and work completion? No! So at the bottom of this very fearful, anxious child's problem was a very suppressive mother who happened to be a colleague from another school. There was no way that I would be able to build a lasting relationship. This year, Jackie's problem continues, only worse. She is with another special education teacher but with the same psychologist asking her to describe her day. The suppressive mother continues to set up her daughter for failure, and she is sinking fast. The mother has lied and snarled communication with the new special education teacher, the new principal, and anyone who gets in her path. The parent is manipulating the special education to serve her own purposes.

Starling was a member of a self-contained class of learning disabled students that I once taught in a middle school. He was terrified of coming to school and leaving his mother and had chalked up enough school absences over the years to get him into a special education class for the severely learning disabled. I suggested to his mother if she could get him to the steps of the school, I would do the rest. She did. I brought him to my classroom, and shortly afterwards he was nauseous and wanted to go to the bathroom. I offered him the trashcan rather than allow him to run off. He sat and looked at it for a spell before attempting his work. Little by little, on a gradient, with his mother bringing him to school and my meeting him at the door of the school, he conquered his school phobia and went on to become quite a successful and delightful student. His problem was that he could not confront the school itself. It was a dangerous environment for him.

On Observation

    A gift you can give yourself and your students that will pay very large dividends in their learning is to teach them to observe; just look at something. This is a fundamental skill for anything that a person is going to do in life. You would be utterly amazed at how difficult it is for a student or anyone else to describe something accurately when the object is no longer present. They even have difficulty describing the object when they are looking at it. It is as though they have blinders on and their perceptions are dulled, which often they are. Lack of this one skill alone is probably the main reason why students are labeled learning disabled. The student was not allowed to construct his own information from the data he found. He was not given an opportunity to apply it. As a result, he became apathetic about education. Eventually, he does not want anything to do with school anymore, but he is forced to accept it, because that is what society tells him. So, he accepts it, but he does not prosper.

    Their perceptions are dulled because somewhere along the line their self-determinism in learning has been violated. You will notice a lot of these students wear glasses, or look but cannot really see. It is often because they do not want to see. They may react to sound but not really discriminate the words. It is sometimes because they have tuned you out by choice. So much information has been forced upon the student without his agreement, his hearing and sight are dulled. Frequently, other senses are dulled, too. And these can be rehabilitated with practice. It is not visual or auditory processing, it is this forced learning coupled with misunderstood vocabulary that contributes to the so-called information-processing deficit of students identified with learning disabilities. This could account for the poor memories that we see in special education. Can you *process* what people say when you have not understood some of the words? Could you process instructions in a foreign language such as German when there are many words you do not understand? Can the student understand the vocabulary in the instructions of the tests given to place him in special classes? Does he choose not to hear?

    A good exercise to improve observation skill is to have students look around the room or out the window, pick an object, and list everything they can experience, using as many perceptions as possible (including weight, height, tactile sensation, personal motion, tone, color, depth perception, emotion and so forth). Then have them look up the name of the object in a good dictionary. Write down the entire definition. Now compare the two writings. They are amazed at how much more information they were able to provide than the dictionary.

I used to teach the profoundly deaf in the beginning of my teaching career, and it was essential to work on many more perceptions than just touch, taste, smell, sight, and residual hearing. We added more perceptions as their language skills improved. For example, they had exercises to learn the weight of an object, its smoothness or roughness, and the feel of movement. They were required to work very hard. Imagine teaching a profoundly deaf person words that are based on sounds like screech and squeal. This training was basic for their learning and interaction in the world around them, helping them to achieve mastery over their environment through communication with the objects and people in it.

Teach observation skills every day and you will see some of these "visual and auditory processing problems" dissolve. First discuss and define observation. Write it on the board. Have the students define perception. Just start with the basics that they know and ease into the others. Make a list and have the students add to it all the ways the body can get information. You will find out that it is more than the five senses we are accustomed to learning. There are many, many ways to gain information. If they cannot observe, they cannot perceive, cannot know, cannot understand, and cannot apply. The glib student knows some things through rote memory but cannot understand and, therefore, cannot apply. He has not learned to observe and perceive. Help the student restore his choice of acceptance by improving his powers of observation. Let him be self-determined on this. Automatically, his memory will improve and so will his acceptance and choice of what he is taught.

Observation is a key to learning about life and people and keeps one in present time. It could even save a life! Observation is a mark of a good scientist, but is it really taught or reinforced? If it is, it is rarely learned, because along the way many of us forget to observe, just look at something and see how it is. It is possible to increase one's observational powers just by defining the different perceptions, one at a time. You will get wonderful results! Just look and observe. This leads students to find out the truth about themselves, others, and their surroundings. It will increase survival potential and put one at cause over his life.

On Reading

The reading instruction I use is based on my observation and research with teaching students with learning disabilities who invariably have deficits in reading. These methods have been improved and revised over the last four years to include word clearing and clay demonstrations. This instruction addresses the so-called problem of developmental dyslexia, a learning disability involving difficulty in learning to read accompanied by erratic spelling and a lack of facility in manipulating written as opposed to spoken words. According to the research, the condition is cognitive in essence and usually genetically determined. Researchers even suggest that it could represent a maturational defect that tends to lessen as the student grows older. Maturity, I agree, is an important consideration, and I have seen it straighten out a lot of problems, but not reading, if they never learned in the first place. I see the problem as one inherent in the method of the teacher and the learning rate of the individual student. These two are rarely addressed because of a basic misunderstanding of what causes a student not to learn in the first place.

After viewing the reading assessment profiles of hundreds of students in special education with reading deficits, I noticed a trend. I saw that there was very often a dip in decoding skills. I had ignored these findings for quite some time because I had been taught in my university course work, as had most of my colleagues teaching secondary students with reading disabilities, to believe that if the student did not *get* decoding by the second grade, he was not likely to *get* it at all. So initially I threw out the idea entirely of teaching decoding to students in sixth grade and beyond. We were taught to teach these students survival skills! But how could they survive with only a smidgen of reading? Once I recall being rather smug when I observed a colleague struggling with teaching sixth-grade students with reading disabilities to decode. I thought, as I had been indoctrinated to think, that this woman was wasting their time and hers. To add to the puzzle of understanding, I had had experience as a teacher of the deaf and noticed that deaf students, even the profoundly deaf, could learn to read without decoding instruction.

It finally dawned on me that deaf students came to the classroom with a solid foundation of the sounds of the language that they had acquired from speech training.

Hearing processing or auditory processing from the annals of learning disability research was someone's opinion, as far as I was concerned, and did not address the problem of teaching a student to read. I still was not clear on what caused the problem, but I no longer cared. I wanted something to *teach* these students to read, something workable. None of the materials, software, and computer equipment, or the expertise of reading teachers had fixed the problems of some of the students that I had begun to encounter at my current high school. I could only rely on myself and my intention that they should read. I began an all-out effort to teach reading when I inherited a group of students who challenged me to teach them anything.

One student was so low that he had become completely apathetic about reading altogether, and he was a senior! I had to act fast! So I began in earnest, using what I knew and could observe from the students, a reading plan that would eventually pay big dividends. I was already in the middle of working on my doctorate and decided then and there that my dissertation would be on reading. I had looked at all the research that I could find on reading, and most of what I found was someone's opinion based on someone else's opinion. I could not find anything that I felt was workable. Finally, I came upon the dyslexic model at Texas Scottish Rite Hospital. I called and spoke to one of the research assistants there, who was mildly interested in my work but not eager enough to give me what I wanted. I realized that the Shriners supported this hospital and thought they might help. Sure enough, I contacted the local masonic lodge and they provided me copies of the videotapes for a relatively small fee. This program would be the foundation for my reading instruction and research treatment. This program was a piece of technology that I could use and think with because it had the entire sequence of reading skills on videotapes, allowing me to control the rate of delivery. I would compare this treatment on vocabulary word acquisition with a computer-based program.

It is important here to mention the definition of dyslexia: simply stated, it means inability to read. The dyslexic definition includes

Learning Disabilities: The Myth

basic problems in learning the alphabet and its phonic properties, word recognition, reading comprehension, writing, copying, and spelling. These students have difficulty with the symbols of written language. The definition describes the deficits the student has — that is about it. It is interesting that we spend a lot of time trying to figure out what deficit a student has, yet give very little time to finding a solution that works. We rarely check to see if the student has any misunderstood words and if he is applying what he has been taught. We become fixed on the label and convinced that something is wrong with the student. So the teacher's intention could be weakened if we follow our university lessons learned.

Undoing wrong lessons learned and providing instruction on the correct gradient and rate take time and patience. Repetition of key words and sounds for long and short vowel sounds and basic vowel patterns, for example, are essential in providing the student a foundation for reading if this step has been skipped in his early years of instruction. Unfortunately, this reading instruction was not enough for Sam, because I got him mid-year of his senior year, and he sat in total apathy for about a month. Eventually, I had to make him angry enough to want to learn to read. That was a tone considerably above where he was, and it took provoking him into reading to get him out of his apathetic state. It was my intention that he read, and he did. He made some gains and, at least, knew when he graduated that there was a way out. Getting a student who is illiterate so late in his schooling makes one wonder what it is we are doing in the field of education. What are we doing in education? Sam could learn to read, but we did not have the time it required. Study is hard work, and material must be delivered on the right gradient and rate for anything to stick. Getting him to define and use to full understanding key words in his job was the best we could accomplish. But it was a start.

Leah, on the other hand, was a tremendous success story! It took three years, though. According to reports from her mother and her, she used to hurl her textbooks across the room because she was so frustrated at not being able to read. I will never forget the first day she walked into the classroom and saw me sitting behind the desk. She glared at me, claws extended, when I greeted her and told her to take a seat. She yelled, "Who do you think you are?" I responded close to her tone, "I am your new teacher, so get in that seat right now!" That was the first and last time she ever barked at me, but she did continue to challenge teachers and other authority figures throughout the school for a while, as she had been accustomed to doing in the past. Slowly and steadily on a gradient, her reading improved and so did her behavior. Teachers now described her as sweet and clever, saying she was a pleasure to teach. Her appearance changed from a bedraggled and dirty looking student with greasy hair to a very attractive and neat young lady, one who took pride in her clothes, hair, and personal hygiene. Her attendance improved greatly along with her motivation to learn. Her grades could only go up from dismal failure, and up they went. She made the honor roll her first quarter in the reading program and learning strategies classes and stayed there for the next three years. She wanted to be part of the group at last and began accepting responsibility for school wide decisions regarding student rules. Although she was not elected, she had the confidence to run for class office, student government and NJROTC princess. She did not give up and even ran for president of her senior class the following year. The suppressive senior class sponsor effectively blocked this because she recalled Leah's past history and did not believe any special education student was capable of leadership. According to her teacher reports and mother, Leah had truly made a dramatic change! Leah knew she had, too. She had only one setback in her senior year when love overtook her. Finally, she could read; the treatment had worked.

Lamar was another big success story! He was diagnosed as severe ADHD with learning disabilities accompanied by intellectual deficits; he even appeared retarded with his shapeless body, sluggish movements and large ears. First of all, students must have at least low-average intelligence to get along in this reading program. However, I noticed that Lamar could do rote math and even solve word problems if the problem was explained, so I doubted the "diagnosis." His tapping and thumping used to drive me crazy: "Please put your pen down, Lamar," I would say, or, "Sit up and listen." I would let him have extra trips to the bathroom just to give us all a break from his fidgeting and annoying behaviors. Finally, as his reading improved, so did his behavior. He was calmer and could sit longer and endure the two classes with me. His understanding was increasing; he was no longer lost in the confusion of misunderstood words and could, therefore, sit for longer periods of time. The first quarter he made the honor roll, he was all puffed up with pride, and his mother was beside herself with joy! She shared that he had been placed in a class with retarded students in the past and she knew deep down that he was not retarded. He certainly was not, though he had looked and behaved as if he were in the beginning of the school year. He was manifesting many of the twenty-six physiological and mental symptoms that accompany a misunderstood word.

As my reading program expanded to include two classes, I added a couple of methods from L. Ron Hubbard's *Basic Study Manual*: word clearing and clay demonstrations. Students were assigned words to define and clarify, using a method of word clearing. The first step is to look up the word, read all the definitions until the correct definition is found, and record the word in their reading journals. Synonyms, word derivations and usage notes are studied. (The precise procedures are given in the text.) Students were encouraged to sketch a picture of the word, if it would help. Next the student would work out the definition of the word in clay through a procedure also in the *Basic Study Manual*. It is amazing to see the light go on when the student has put together a clay demonstration of the word. If the word is not described clearly, the demonstration is flunked and worked at until it is correct. The observer must be able to look at the demonstration and know what the word is. Every separate part of the clay demonstration is labeled with one-word labels from slips of stiff paper, such as 3 x 5 cards. The vocabulary word being defined is the first word written and turned face down in front of the model. The teacher must be able to understand the demonstration before reading the word.

DeVonn joined my reading class this year at the beginning of third quarter. He is an eighth-grader, and the reading teacher from the middle school was getting desperate for help. She had already requested that I work with him last year when he made no progress, but my principal refused and said I had enough on my plate already. This year I took him in. As a prerequisite, I asked the reading teacher and learning disability teacher to write down what had been tried with a statement that it did not work. This done, I requested permission from my principal. Finally, I asked my colleagues to stop all interventions at their school to see if what I offered would take. I said that we would need about a quarter before we could measure any progress.

The other school had tried a computer-based reading program that is all the rage with our system right now. I might add that it cost hundreds of thousands of dollars to send teachers to Hawaii for the training, purchase of more computers and software, and installation of the software. The reading teacher stated that DeVonn had made very little progress with this program because he "was so low with spelling and word recognition." She stated that he had been in self-contained reading classes for all three years at the middle school. She mentioned that he had had individual tutoring by the elementary school principal one summer, and that he had been working with the school psychologist with a phonics-based reading program for about a year. Still he had made no progress. I put him on the study gradient, which was quite low because he was completely illiterate, and then we proceeded. I made a mental note that when DeVonn made a clay demonstration of net with a fith (fish) in it, he did not understand the consonant digraph sh. By the end of the fourth session, he read an entire page of words independently to his amazement and the sincere acknowledgment and spontaneous applause of other students in the class. When his sponsor returned from Iraq recently, he could see that his nephew was finally learning to read at the age of fifteen. He, therefore, demanded and got another reading class with me because the method used worked. DeVonn is on his way to literacy!

Chandra was also in my reading class as well as another support class called Learning Strategies. I found out rather quickly that she did not understand a great deal of the words she was using; it was just parrot speech. And she got into a whole lot of trouble for what spewed forth from her mouth due to her lack of understanding. She was loud, sassy, and challenged nearly every word her teachers spoke if she was not in agreement when she had been directed to do something, always adding that she would tell her momma on them. No one wanted her in their classes, not only because she was way, way below grade level in everything but because of her attitude

Learning Disabilities: The Myth

and total ignorance of the fact that anyone else was present. By her second year in our high school, the very stern NJROTC colonel ordered her to "Get out!" when she showed up for his class again. His method of discipline had not worked, and he was clearly fed up. One day at the beginning of her first year in my class, I told her, "Be quiet, Chandra!" She continued her side conversations and laughter. Then in a firmer voice, I reminded her, "I gave you a command. Be quiet, now!" She raised her voice and shouted, "You cannot give me a command. I'm gonna tell my momma!" To which I replied, "Yes, I can," then I realized she did not have the definition for command. Well, we discussed command as it pertained to types of sentences and practiced some drills until she finally got it. Another time, when we were discussing some simple and easy words, unashamedly she asked in front of everyone, "Does below mean down?" We cleared the word together, and she felt more at ease. Chandra epitomizes the student who could decode words but did not have a clue or interest even in their meaning. She had been passed along from one special reading group to the next, and her undefined words mounted. Most recently, she had exited a computerized reading program that she thoroughly enjoyed but still had no comprehension of what she was reading unless it was the most basic and simplistic of sentences. No wonder she had no interest in school, other than the social life.

During about my fourth year of teaching, when I was teaching in a middle school in Georgia, I had a self-contained class for severe learning-disabled students. There was a student I will call Karen who was probably in the class only because of her extreme shyness. Her face would turn red if you asked her a question, and the response that followed was nearly inaudible. She was a very pretty little girl and always did her work and needed very little help. I recall one day thinking to myself, "I will listen to this girl read and find out if she really does have any type of reading problem that I can see." I gave her a copy of the basal reader for seventh grade, and she selected a story. I asked her to read it with me, and we proceeded. I could barely hear her at all at first but continued reading, stopping intermittently to ask her a few questions that she answered softly. Finally, over the course of the next days and weeks, I faded my voice, very, very slowly. In about two months, she could read aloud if I would start her, and so the gradient continued over the year until she was reading alone.

Why did this reading instruction work? Because I intended it to work in the first place. Intention is basic to getting the outcome you want. It is my belief that all students can learn; it is their rate of learning that makes the difference, not the quantity that they can hold in their heads that defines their knowledge base. It is not some processing problem or emotional issue, or lack of motivation or intelligence. It is wrong lessons learned that must be unlearned that are causing the lags in learning. Some students learn quickly and well with little instruction. (This answered the question for me why some profound deaf students were able to learn language, read, and speak without hearing the sounds of the language.) Others have lags in learning and require more repetition and drill; they move slower. These students need a lower study gradient, mass (such as clay or blocks or the real thing), and clearing of their misunderstood words. As a matter of fact, all students should be placed on a study gradient and progress at their own pace.

Reading taught at the correct gradient for each student by using the correct study technology could cure the ills of all the splinter groups of students in education. Students are not allowed to pass a word that has been misunderstood. There is plenty of repetition and drill for mastery. Students are taught the rules and drill, taught the symbols and drill. Literature and poetry are brought in on a gradient with clearing up misunderstood words. Spelling and writing are drilled. Do not assume that students can read or make all the cursive letters, even in high school, because they cannot. All parts of reading and grammar are broken into basic units, rehearsed, and drilled over and over again. They must have ample opportunities to have mass to assist understanding of words until mastery is achieved. When mastery is achieved, the student can then become self-determined about study because he can then apply what he has learned. And application is the only reason to learn something in the first place.

On Writing

Producing effective and interesting written expression can be an overwhelming task for students with disabilities who have had a history of failure. Teaching the writing process approach to these students has been demonstrated to be an effective strategy for increasing the production and quality of students' writing. This does not come easy for a student with learning disabilities in reading and written language. However, students can learn to write by confronting writing. The student must move on a gradient and must always be self-determined. (Information in this chapter is based on the following article with permission from the authors: Marchisan, M. L., Alber, S. R. 2001. "The Write Way: Tips for Teaching the Writing Process to Resistant Writers," *Intervention in School and Clinic* 36: 154-161.)

Written expression is probably the most difficult skill to teach because it is the most complex form of communication. All of us must write in some form or another throughout our lives, but somewhere along the way many of us learn to detest writing. In school we have been bribed, cajoled, and sometimes threatened into writing about contrived topics that have no personal relevance and no real audience. Dull and flat writing results from generic story starters or suggestions to write about vacations or family pets. (Some students are even given writing assignments as a form of punishment!) What is the consequence of all of this hard work? A returned paper marked up with red ink magnifying each error.

Teachers can cause roadblocks to writing without even realizing it when they use dittos and canned starters for writing. It is important to understand that students will write and will care about writing when it is personal. They come to school with a repertoire of experiences, concerns, and ideas waiting to be written. These students can benefit from the writing workshop approach because writing is self-determined, is on a gradient scale, and the writer has a computer and lots of stimulus stories, films, or experiences to provide mass. Discussions and brainstorming help in the prewriting stage. Further, the student extends his vocabulary by the clarification and use of new words.

Thomas: A Resistant Writer

By the time Thomas, a student with learning disabilities, had reached seventh grade, he had a history of academic failure. Patterns of disruptive behaviors and helplessness were firmly ingrained. Thomas was demanding to be heard but did not have the skills to express himself either orally or through written expression. He could not communicate. Thomas changed dramatically over the next three years. His metamorphosis came in the form of overcoming the barriers that had blocked his writing and learning in general. With the writing process approach, Thomas learned to express himself and to experience success. As Thomas confronted writing, he began doing it. He realized that there was an audience out there who could appreciate his ideas, and he grew and blossomed as a student and a writer as a result. It was a gradual process along a bumpy road that took him to a freeway of smooth, rich expression. The implementation of the writing process paved the way.

The writing process stresses student ownership and self-determinism as written expression develops and matures through specific activities used in the following stages: prewriting, writing, revising, and publishing. Some practical strategies teachers may use through the stages of the writing process are presented here.

The Prewriting Stage

In the prewriting stage, students think about and plan what they will write by focusing on the following important decisions: Why am I writing (purpose)? What will I write about (subject)? What will I say (content)? How will I say it (voice)? For whom am I writing (audience)?

The first step of prewriting is motivating students to think about specific topics of personal interest. This can be accomplished by encouraging students to talk about their heroes such as favorite athletes, musicians, or television and film personalities. Students may also be encouraged to talk about favorite activities such as building model cars, collecting comic books, origami, cooking, or playing computer games. Students can be encouraged to write a piece describing procedures for doing their favorite activities. If students are reluctant to talk about their interests, teachers may discover student interests through observation during free-choice activities. What kind of books does the student select during free reading time? What does the student like to talk about with his peers? What kind of pictures does the student like to draw? The teacher can use the student's specific interests to motivate written expression.

A light went on for Thomas when he was encouraged to write about the Middle Ages, dungeons, dragons, and knights. Thomas loved to talk about his interest in the Dungeons & Dragons role-playing game series. Literature and films related to the Middle Ages were used to stimulate Thomas's interest. In particular, he enjoyed discussing warfare in the Middle Ages and developed a vast knowledge of weapons and armor. When history lessons or literature stories linked to this period in history, Thomas enthusiastically participated and shared his growing body of knowledge. Once Thomas showed a strong interest in a particular topic, it was a relatively easy transition to get him to put his thoughts down on paper. Thomas will probably never exhaust his repertoire of stories about the Middle Ages, but he was able to move on to writing about other topics as well. Thomas was self-determined on this topic and could apply what he had learned!

Use Recall of Perceptions. Teachers can facilitate the student's recall of background experiences by stimulating visual imagery and perceptions. For example, "The First House Memory" is an exercise in which the students close their eyes and visualize a room in a house where they experienced a holiday or memorable event. They are led through the house room by room as the teacher gently guides them to recall the details, the smells, the touch and weight of familiar objects, the sights and sounds outside the window. Afterward, students draw a floor plan of the house with as many details as possible. Then they write two to three sentences about one of these rooms and discuss why it was memorable.

Other examples of perceptual experiences and recall include having the student imagine walking on a hot, sandy beach and jumping in the cool ocean, being knocked over by a wave, and tasting the salty water on a hot summer day; walking through the woods and feeling the crunch of leaves under his feet and the cool, crisp air on his cheeks on an autumn day; or sliding down a wet, grassy hill in the springtime and listening to the chirp of the birds and the buzz of the bees. The student can generate his own list of adjectives related to these pictures he recalled. Thus, training observation skills through exercises with perceptions helps free up the writer and enables him to add important details in his writing necessary for communication with his audience.

Model Prewriting Procedures. An effective way to help students determine the purpose, audience, and tone of their writing is through demonstration. The teacher may begin by selecting a topic of his own personal interest and thinking aloud while brainstorming ideas and placing them in a story web, map, or outline. After this prewriting procedure has been demonstrated, the teacher can guide students to brainstorm and develop their own story plans.

Once students are motivated to write about a specific topic, the teacher should model prewriting strategies such as brainstorming, clustering, and self-questioning strategies (who? what? where? when? why? and how?). Thomas's teacher began by modeling a brainstorming and mapping technique on the board after a group discussion of a topic. It is important to remind students to avoid evaluating or clarifying their ideas during the brainstorming stage. When Thomas's teacher worked with him individually, she allowed him to dictate his ideas while she wrote them on a story map. Before long, Thomas was able to construct his own story maps. Later on, this translated to the computer.

- Narrative story writing. While planning the content of a narrative story, have students use the W-W-W, What-2, How-2 strategy:
  Who (is the main character)?
  When (does it take place)?
  Where (does it take place)?

What (does the main character want to do)?
What (happens when she does it)?
How (does it end)?
How (does the character feel)?

- Opinion essays. Place students with a partner and tell them to take opposite sides of an issue (e.g., we should increase the lunch break at our high school), generate two or three arguments to support their opinions, write down their ideas, and discuss their arguments with their partners. Students may then use their notes to write their opinion essays. I have found that using children's literature provides a wealth of ideas for students to use in persuasive writing. Pair up students or divide the class into two groups and role-play the good-versus-evil themes in a story, then swap sides. (This can be a lot of fun.) It helps the student see the other's point of view and increases his ability to argue both sides.

- Compare and contrast essays. Have the students work with partners to select a topic and two categories of the topic to compare and contrast (e.g., economical junior prom in the school cafeteria versus an expensive junior prom at an elegant hotel.) For each feature selected, students list details and descriptive vocabulary. The students then use the compare and contrast plan to write their essays.

- Analytical compositions. Prior to writing an analytical composition about a story the students have read, have students: (a) self-question (e.g., Who is the story about? Where does the story take place? What is the problem in the story?); (b) complete a story map that prompts students to write the character, setting, problems, events, and solutions for the story they read; (c) use a chart to fill in information about elements of the story

The Writing Stage

During the writing stage, the student writes sentences and paragraphs that expound on his prewriting notes. When writing a first draft, the student should focus on sequential expression of content without regard to the mechanical aspects of writing. Mechanics are to be addressed during the revision stage. If the student is overly concerned about spelling, grammar, and punctuation at the writing stage, his writing fluency may be inhibited.

Word Banks. To assist students in the clear expression of their ideas, the teacher may want to provide students with various types of word banks. Adjective and verb word banks can be used to make student products more descriptive and interesting. Students may also develop individualized word banks of self-selected words they frequently use in their writing. Always have on hand a good student dictionary so the student becomes practiced in extending his vocabulary and becomes very familiar with the new words. He must demonstrate a clear understanding of his words, their different definitions, derivations, synonyms, and usage. He then becomes more fluent and literate. Move slowly and precisely here or he will not maintain the words and will not be able to apply the words with complete accuracy later on.

Promote Fluency. Deficits in writing fluency can make written expression a tedious chore. To promote fluency, the teacher should incorporate as much written expression as possible in other content areas throughout the school day. Writing in a personal journal at the same time every day on a self-selected topic may extend fluency as well. If students have difficulty thinking of a topic, the teacher may suggest topics that evoke strong emotions such as school regulations, curfews, allowances, or homework.

Another way to promote fluency is by requiring repeated writings and timing students to see how many words they can write in one minute. For example, the teacher may discuss or read a story to students and have them write down as many details as they can remember. The details students jot down can then be used as notes

Learning Disabilities: The Myth

for timed writings. Keeping a words-per-minute chart that shows student improvement can be very motivating to the reluctant writer.

Allow Students to Write at the Computer. Thomas had motor difficulties and could work much more rapidly at the computer. He had not mastered cursive handwriting and his printing was large and laborious. He even reached a point where he would choose to throw out his story and start over entirely with a new idea. Word processing programs allow students to cut and paste and make frequent revisions without the necessity of recopying. Having the visibility of the text on the screen can be useful for facilitating collaborative writing between peers and when necessary, with the teacher.

Use a Co-writing Strategy. Co-writing a story with the teacher provides the student with a more supportive model for written expression and can be an effective strategy for students who have extreme difficulty putting a story together. Good communication with affinity and agreement must be in place for this to work; otherwise, the student is going to reject this close proximity of help. Thomas sat beside the teacher at the computer as the teacher took Thomas's kernel of an idea from his story map and typed it on the screen. Next, she questioned him. He provided some very sketchy information as she began to write. Initially, Thomas was content to sit beside the teacher and answer questions as she probed for more information about his story. She filled in some gaps and modeled how a story would begin and end. Gradually, Thomas was able to fill in more parts of his story independently. After the teacher, using Thomas's ideas, modeled several stories, he became self-determined and took over ownership of his work completely.

Gradually Fade Your Assistance. Be available, but begin to fade your assistance slowly as soon as the student shows an inclination to write independently. Fade on a gradient in stages. Fade the ending first, then the middle, and finally, the beginning, or use whatever works. Eventually, Thomas had his story in mind and began using his brainstorming cluster and at the same time, cleared his misunderstood words as he increased the length of his vocabulary words and sentences. He only required assistance for grammar and sentence structure. It is important for teachers to provide encouragement by acknowledging improvement in the student's writing skills.

The Revision Stage

During the revision stage, students evaluate their own strengths and weaknesses of the form and content of their writing piece and make changes based on these judgments. The teacher never makes evaluative statements. This stage of the writing process requires students to see their drafts as the intended audience might. The following strategies may be especially useful with students who need extra support.

Teach Mini-Lessons. Direct instruction of writing skills should be used at this point to promote effective error correction. The teacher can begin the daily writing period by providing a short lesson (five to ten minutes) of specific writing skills. Analysis of student writing for the most frequent types of errors will help the teacher select appropriate daily lesson topics (e.g., using quotation marks, subject-verb agreement, parallel construction). Because there are so many elements to effective writing, students may find the task of editing their work overwhelming. For this reason, teachers should emphasize only a few writing skills at a time. For example, the teacher may require students to edit their work for capitalization or punctuation errors only. Once students become proficient with a few mechanical editing skills, the teacher can gradually increase the requirements. In other words, they must clear up any misunderstanding about words such as subject, verb, or quotations. Have them model these in clay at the clay table or use a demonstration kit to increase understanding. Grammar and punctuation rules are always difficult for students with deficits because of their misunderstood words.

To demonstrate editing procedures, the teacher may want to use student writing samples at the overhead projector (without names) that need revision in a certain area. The teacher and students collaboratively edit the writing piece together. The teacher may also want to show samples of revised drafts, provide copies for students, and discuss the changes that were made. Have students suggest any other revisions that may be appropriate and explain why. It is also important for the teacher to share her own writing pieces and the struggles that were experienced with some part of the composition.

Provide a Self-Evaluation Checklist. To guide students through the revision process, provide students with a list of questions to answer as they read through their first draft (see Figures 1 and 2). These questions may guide students through the evaluation of the content, organization, and style of their drafts. Students with disabilities should probably focus on a lower gradient and address content first. When responding to the questions on the self-evaluation checklist, students should be taught to write notes on their drafts as they evaluate. Their notes can then be used to write the next revision. Because Thomas needed extra practice using the self-evaluation checklists, his teacher provided him with models of writing samples and their corresponding checklists. Thomas used these models as a reference tool when practicing the evaluation of other writing samples. This exercise was valuable in assisting Thomas with evaluating his own work.

Encourage Voice. When encouraging students to elaborate on their ideas, the teacher should also encourage voice. Ask students to describe the voice of the characters, and have them role-play if necessary. Ask if there is a real personality behind the voice. Are all the characters distinct individuals? What needs to be done to individualize each character? Let students know that their ideas and ways of expressing themselves are important. The teacher may want to write with the student at the computer as he reads through the piece and type his responses so that the flow of ideas will not be interrupted.

Use Conferencing. Conferences with students about their writing should be brief, about five to ten minutes, depending on the student's needs. Teacher conferences may be conducted throughout each stage of the writing process. During these conferences, it is important that the teacher has good communication with the student. Through questioning, the teacher can help the student gain more insight into his own ideas and self-expression. The teacher should listen and offer suggestions when asked. Allow the student to be self-determined about his writing. Thomas was very dependent on the teacher in the early stages of his writing. If he did not get what he determined was his share of attention, he became disruptive and demanded attention in other, inappropriate ways. Each student should have at least one writing conference with the teacher per week. Allow students to sign up for conference times so they know when they can count on receiving individual attention. During conferences, the teacher should point out the strengths of a writing piece before noting problems. When problems are addressed, the teacher and student should collaboratively solve them.

Praise Student Gains. Many students with learning disabilities have experienced years of frustration with written expression by the time they reach middle and high school, and Thomas was no exception. In addition to his academic deficits, he had social problems as well. As his writing skills increased and his ideas took shape, Thomas's behavior also improved. He felt validated for his gains and could see the results himself in a story he had produced. Teachers must be aware of the gains the student makes on a gradient scale, as well as the effort.

Use Peer-Editing Partners or Groups. By discussing how to develop, evaluate, revise, and proofread each other's drafts, students can gain valuable insight into their own and their classmates' writing processes. Students also gain insight into the role of the audience. The teacher is a guide who watches for problems and intervenes when appropriate. Most importantly, the teacher ensures that there is a classroom atmosphere of trust and cooperation. This is critical if students like Thomas are to succeed.

Allow students to exchange papers with a partner and find the strengths and weaknesses in each other's drafts. Remind them that authors always have editors or someone who reads the writing before it is published. Also, tell them that few writers are able to identify the

Learning Disabilities: The Myth

strengths and weaknesses in a single draft. Once students become more skilled at working with one partner, the teacher may want to move the student to another peer-editing group.

Students need guidance in accepting feedback from others. If they have been trained in good communication skills, then the students will know not to evaluate for the writer or tell him what to think. Instead, the peer editor will question the writer about his work and show him examples of good construction of sentences.

Provide Guidance for Revising a Draft. Teachers should emphasize to students that revising a draft means to improve it, to look for ways to help the paper achieve its purpose for a particular audience in an even better way, and not for the sake of just making changes. Help students understand that revision takes time and effort. Important writing and thinking are often done at this stage of the writing process. Be patient. The ability to revise improves on a gradient and comes with practice and writing.

When making revisions, the writer becomes a problem solver. Although revision takes time, working at a computer with a word processor can reduce the tedium of handwriting for students with motor difficulties like Thomas. Students with disabilities need help in understanding that revision is not recopying. Revision is examining suggestions, selecting those that make sense, elaborating, and adding details or clarifying an idea or theme. Evaluation is finding parts that are unclear and weak. Students should keep samples of good writing in their writing folders, which give them a standard of reference. When Thomas worked on a piece that was guided too heavily by the teacher, he tore up the draft and developed a story of his own that went on for pages and even chapters. He had developed ownership and suddenly realized what it felt like to create and become an author. This proved to be a turning point for Thomas because he was now self-determined about his writing.

TEACH STUDENTS TO USE THE COMPUTER FOR EDITING. Teach students to add, cut, reorder, and replace. This can be accomplished quite easily at the computer. Students who are on a slow gradient benefit from the teacher's modeling how to make revisions at the computer. Suggestions for revision should include reordering ideas that may confuse the reader and revising the content to include additional important details. Students should remember to be sure that the details support the main idea. Remind students to revise for organization and make sure that ideas are presented and connected in a clear and logical way. Make sure students also revise for word choice and that the words are appropriate for the intended audience. Show students how to substitute more vivid, precise, and appropriate vocabulary. Make sure that students save their stories on their hard drive at home.

PROVIDE GUIDANCE FOR PROOFREADING A REVISED DRAFT. When proofreading a revised draft, the writer rereads his writing and corrects grammar, usage, and other mechanical errors. Thomas was able to self-correct much of his writing, but he was never able to catch all his spelling errors or punctuation mistakes. It worked best to have Thomas sit beside the special education teacher at the computer and talk through the grammar corrections. Thomas and his teacher examined the writing piece line by line together. This approach taught Thomas to examine his work more carefully and clear up his misunderstood words and improve his grammar.

Provide a checklist for students to use when proofreading the mechanics of their revised drafts. A checklist may be developed individually by collaborating with the student to address his most frequent problems (see Figure 3). Students should not be held responsible for skills that they have not been taught. However, they should be taught skills on a gradient as used. It will take more time and supervision for some students. Frequently, finding the correct spelling of a word can be very frustrating. For example, if a student does not know the digraph sh, he may spell fith instead of fish.

Writing a final version involves preparing a clean copy of a revised and proofread paper. The writer should follow the standards for correct manuscript form or specific instructions for the paper. Students should be reminded that messy, torn papers discourage readers. Remind students to proofread their final versions once again before giving the paper to the intended audience.

KEEP A WRITING PORTFOLIO. Students should keep their stories and compositions in a writing folder or portfolio so that the teacher and student can monitor progress. Earlier writing pieces can be compared to current ones so that students can see the gains they have made over time. Writing pieces are permanent products that can also be used at IEP (individualized education plan) meetings to document progress and plan future instruction. By analyzing the work kept in the portfolio, the student can help choose goals for future pieces of writing.

Publishing and Sharing Writing

The emphasis during this stage of the writing process should be to improve the appearance and the ease of reading, as well as promote pride in authorship. Students need the opportunity to publish and share their writing with others to determine its effect on real audiences. Teachers can publish student writing in the following ways:

- Display compositions on hallway or classroom bulletin boards or in the form of artwork such as collages and mobiles.
- Have students construct books complete with illustrations to put on display in the classroom or library.
- Schedule a regular time for the "author's chair" and allow students to volunteer to read their pieces with the entire class or small groups.
- Submit student work to children's magazines and local or school newspapers.
- Create a classroom newsletter, newspaper, or magazine.
- Use the Internet for collaborative writing and publishing with students from other geographical areas.
- Have students make audiotapes of their writing complete with sound effects, and make the tapes available to students in the class, school, and community.
- Have students produce a videotape of a story or play they have written, and allow classmates to play the different characters.

Resistant writers can be taught to write using the writing process approach paired with the tools of study technology, direct instruction, and a committed, well-trained teacher. Students like Thomas can become contributing members of the classroom when teachers employ patience, good communication, support, and frequent opportunities for writing and sharing. Students can be trained to be astute observers using all their perceptions in writing exercises that can then be translated in to a finished product. Thomas evolved academically and socially over the next three years while learning to express himself through writing. By the end of the ninth grade, he had calmed down considerably and found a new purpose and meaning in school and life. He developed a sense of humor, friendships with his peers, and he even had a girlfriend. Thomas grew with his writing and gained confidence as he learned to express his ideas in print and share them with an audience. Many factors probably contributed to Thomas's newfound confidence. Slowly, he learned and practiced good communication with his teacher, and realized help was available. Through this communication, he saw that he *himself* could exercise control over his *own* writing, thereby translating his ideas onto a blank page. He had become self-determined over his learning and was able to express himself in writing. He had become a member of the community of learners!

Title_____

Author_____

Date_____

Peer Editor_____

____ **Is the beginning interesting?**

____ **Does the story make sense?**

____ **Are the characters believable? Do they act like real people?**

____ **Do the characters use conversation?**

____ **Are the characters' personalities developed?**

____ **Does the story have a problem that needs to be solved?**

____ **Are the descriptions of the scenes clear?**

____ **Does each scene build toward the high point (climax) in the story?**

____ **Is there an exciting or high point of the story?**

____ **Is the conclusion logical? Does it wrap up all the loose ends?**

____ **Was the conflict or problem resolved?**

____ **Was there a moral or theme?**

Figure 1. Checklist for revising fiction.

Marta L Marchisan, Ph D

Title_____

Author_____

Date_____

Peer Editor_____

____ **Has the author written for a particular audience?**

____ **Has the author written for a specific purpose?**

____ **Does the introduction of the piece get the reader involved right away?**

____ **Are the ideas developed in a logical sequence?**

____ **Does the author stay on topic?**

____ **Are the ideas clear?**

____ **Are there details to support the main ideas?**

____ **Is correct grammar used?**

____ **Are words spelled correctly?**

____ **Is there a surprise ending or strong conclusion?**

Figure 2. Checklist for revising nonfiction.

Personal Editing Checklist

Use this checklist to edit your work for mechanical errors.

Does every sentence have an end punctuation mark?
   periods for telling sentences   _____
   question marks for asking sentences   _____
   exclamation marks for sentences that show
   strong emotion   _____

Are periods used with abbreviations?   _____

Are commas used correctly?
   for lists
   for dates   _____
   to separate phrases   _____
   between city and state   _____
   after direct address   _____

Are semicolons used correctly?   _____
   to join independent clauses in a sentence

Are colons used correctly?
   to set off a list   _____
   for time   _____

Are quotation marks used correctly for conversation?   _____

Are subject and verb in agreement?   _____

Are proper nouns and the beginning of sentences capitalized?   _____

Is the spelling correct?   _____

Are apostrophes used correctly?
   for possessive nouns   _____
   for contractions   _____

Figure 3. Editing checklist

On Math

I once had a professor say that the "IEPs are fictional garbage!" It startled me at the time but I never forgot what he said. Much of what I get from other schools and also am required to select from the computer banks of goals and objectives is fiction and can be thrown in the waste bin. I learned early on to observe a student, forget about the IEP, and start from there. The student would tell me what I needed to know. Once I have done all the preliminary work on a student's case, I never look at his history again. I do not need it.

Jamie Jon's Individual Education Plan on math was no exception. He had a huge file with all the medical documents and tests about his multiple handicaps, which included autism. What I needed to know was what he could do in math in order for me to teach him. That is all I wanted to know. There were a number of goals about division and computation and so on. I found out right away he had not understood any of this, could not subtract, and was rather shaky with addition. He could not apply for certain. What did I do? I backed up again and again and again. I was looking for the correct gradient!

Jamie Jon and I found his gradient at the very foundation of math. He needed to know the purpose of math and learn that it was sequential. He needed to find the rhythm of math, although Jamie Jon had no rhythm himself. He always dragged his feet when he walked and would engage in other self-stimulating behaviors. He had no affect and would laugh inappropriately. It was not even a real laugh, it was mimicry; for example, he would tell a Rodney Dangerfield joke and then laugh as if on cue. Jamie Jon was not very attractive physically; he wore braces and had acne, a cleft lip, and hair that could not be tamed and laid every which way. He also had severe learning problems. He could read some and get literal meaning to about a fifth- or sixth-grade level, but had no higher order interpretation or evaluation of what it was he had read, or so it appeared. He rarely initiated any type of communication, other than with me and, only seldom with the aide that was assigned to him. The aide later told me that he repulsed her and I am sure he sensed it.

I initiated a project with Jamie Jon to teach him math using Unifix Cubes and so set up various patterns for representing numbers and sets. We based the math lessons for several weeks on patterning. But first we did a couple of sessions on just snapping and clapping to get rhythm understood. After he became more expert at this, I called in a film crew (students from a video course) and began to have the sessions filmed, with his and his mother's permission. This film was to be used for the instruction of teachers in a math methods course that I was taking. The way I got his attention and cooperation for each segment was to allow him to tell one of his Rodney Dangerfield jokes. The jokes were outrageous and dirty for the most part, but it worked. I suggested that he call the name of the teacher, "Hey, Ms. Henderson, I got a joke for you." Then he proceeded to tell his very risqué joke, followed by a flat, robotic laugh, devoid of any emotion. My intention was to edit out all the jokes after I shared the film with my colleagues in the course. In the end, we gave Jamie Jon a copy of the film and a copy to the library for instructional purposes. Jamie Jon thought that he was a film star and asked for a copy to send his dad in the States.

The really remarkable thing was Jamie Jon's discovery about math at the end of the three-week session of classes and filming. He looked right into the camera when I asked him, "Jamie Jon, is there anything that you would like to say to the teachers about math?" Without hesitation, he replied, "Math has patterns and rhythm just like the world!" Then he laughed robotically. I was astounded by his discovery!

Students with math problems always have misunderstood words and symbols; most have computation problems. For instance, I had a number of students in Geometry this term and nearly all were failing. Why? Geometry is loaded with vocabulary that seems like a foreign language to the student if he has been allowed to squeak by in Algebra I, using his calculator without understanding, and doing problems by rote. They do need rote memory work but with comprehension. Facts can and should be drilled and drilled until committed to memory. For a while there was the school of thought, especially in special education, that said if the student did not get the facts early on, give him a calculator. Give him a calculator, but drill him on the facts to mastery and using the calculator, if you wish. Students need to work out in clay or blocks their understanding of addition, subtraction, multiplication, and division. Students must demonstrate that they understand words such as minus, plus, addition, subtraction, multiplication, and division. Frequently, the simple words in English and math are the ones most misunderstood. It is not the big new terms, necessarily, that are confusing. These simple words have been compounded through the years to an overwhelming level of stupidity for the student by the time he reaches high school. Therefore, students need to demonstrate that they know all the meanings of the symbols of math as well as the terms, simple and complex. When the student becomes hung up at a higher level, it is because he went past something he misunderstood earlier, and the confusion snowballs. For instance, those seemingly simple phrases like less than, more than, greater than can really impede a student's progress if not fully understood.

There are other reasons why students do not do well in math. Lara had an erratic pattern of doing her Algebra problems. Her computation errors did not make sense. Sometimes she did the problems flawlessly; other times she made simple mistakes throughout an assignment. Some learned folks would say this is merely a characteristic of a student with learning disabilities in math. Their theory is that one day they have it, the next day, they do not. We are trained to the label and often do not look beyond at the obvious. Finally, I sat beside her one day, and we went through the page of problems, step by step. I called her on a couple of careless errors, and she admitted that she could not see the numbers very clearly. Of course, she already had a prescription for glasses but had many excuses for not wearing them. Now she brings her glasses and wears them for math. Although it is very helpful when the school nurse checks the vision of all the students yearly, and then notifies the faculty of those with vision problems, this does not mean that the student has gotten glasses or contact lenses and will wear them. It takes constant vigilance on our part and the parents to see that the student is prepared to learn before we can begin.

Each student or table of students should have at hand a container of various sizes of blocks and be required to demonstrate concepts and words from word problems. Clay is best for defining concepts and working out word problems. Anything can be worked out in clay. If the clay demonstration is well done, then the student will remember the data. They must have an understanding of the concept of numbers, the importance of math in their lives, and be able to apply these facts. They must learn at the very foundation of math and use mass. I suggest clay, if available, for slower students because it lends itself to manipulation. Math basics must be taught on a gradient, the correct gradient for each student. The student must learn thoroughly the basic skills and vocabulary of math to 100-percent mastery. This is the only way that the student will be able to apply.

Another strategy that I am working on with students in various math classes is helping them understand the key terms. This is going to take some cooperation from the regular class teachers, because it takes extra time. For example, Melanie is an excellent student, all around, but she suffers from misunderstood words and, given the pace of the gradient of her Geometry class, has begun to fail the tests. Last year, she was hailed as the top Algebra I student in all the algebra classes, so you can imagine her disappointment. I asked her, "What can we do to solve this problem?" She said, "I get lost on the instructions. If the teacher would give me a list of the instructions before the test, I could learn the words and do better." That is just what we did, and she *did* do better.

Then there was John, a high school junior, who never could understand why he felt so foolish in math; in fact, he felt stupid. Once his area of deficiency was identified and his misunderstanding of the subject was revealed, he was able to proceed. He had misunderstood division, so we backtracked to subtraction until all his misunderstood words and false data were found. There are at least ten ways to misunderstand a word, and we, as teachers, need to know this, and teach it to our students. John progressed so well after learning his basic subtraction facts and division, then clearing his misunderstood words as he went along, that he eventually became quite successful in all his subjects, including math, and went on to college. His mother wrote me later that John had graduated from college, married, and was doing very well.

About twelve years ago, our system started an excellent program of training for teachers on the New Math Standards. All the information known to man had doubled in the previous ten years, therefore, the stress was to get away from shopkeeper math and prepare students for the new age of technology. There were summer training programs and leadership training for the different grade levels and teachers. Trained teachers took the knowledge back to local schools to train other teachers. New equipment was purchased with lots of manipulatives and calculators. Working in cooperative learning groups was in vogue. Teachers were excited, and so were students. The emphasis was on *applying* the math! There were probably some weaknesses such as too much focus on group learning and not enough accountability for the individual learning. And, perhaps, there may have been too much reliance on calculators, and not enough on estimation and learning basic calculations. Nevertheless, this was a great initiative. Slowly, all this knowledge faded because it was not used or reinforced. New teachers came and were not trained. Old teachers were not retrained and checked on their usage and understanding so they could pass the knowledge along. District leaders and our national leaders retired or changed jobs, so no one was left to carry on the torch. Someone new took over and decided to leave his footprint. All this money and effort wasted, down the tube. New leader, new program. Millions more spent on another initiative and with limited gain. And Johnny *still* can't do math.

On Communication

All students with learning problems have communication problems. That means that they are not in communication with themselves, their environment, subjects of study or others for one reason or another. Often the adults in their vicinity, including the teacher, suffer from the same malady. It is not as described in the textbooks: visual and auditory processing, long-term and short-term memory and retrieval deficits. It is simply impaired communication. Why? No one ever had a look at what the problem truly was and tried to address it. Instead, the field was content to use all the esoteric assessment language in special education because it sounded so wise, yet never helped anyone. Recognize that most of us suffer from communication problems because we have not been trained in the proper communication cycle. First we study a good definition of communication and learn some very precise procedures for communication, then practice over and over the correct application. Communication means to express oneself in such a way that one is readily and clearly understood. It means to have an interchange of ideas. (*Second College Edition: The American Heritage Dictionary*, Houghton Mifflin, c. 1991). This implies giving and receiving information. In order to communicate effectively, one must know how to deliver and receive a communication effectively. One must be able to communicate with the subjects of study, the school, teachers, peers, and one's self.

Communication is probably the singularly most important thing we do as teachers, yet little attention is paid to it. Were you ever taught communication as a course in school? How can we teach it, if *we* were not taught it? We cannot! Communication must be taught! Yet, the only class that I have ever seen that approaches communication is a speech class or drama class offered as an elective. The focus is generally elocution and diction, and it is a fun way to get a good grade, but it is not about making you and your ideas understood. If the teacher could communicate her ideas more effectively so that they are duplicated and understood, imagine what the outcome would be. We can do something about this communication void in our own training. We can learn thoroughly the definition of communication, we can read about it and learn all we can about it. Then, apply it.

First, look around you and observe people as they try to express themselves. Just the other day, a colleague stopped me in the hall as I was rushing by, because she had something very important to tell me. Twenty seconds into the conversation, she began to look around and pay attention elsewhere as I attempted to give her the answer. I just stopped in mid-sentence and left; she never even noticed. A similar incident with a male colleague occurred a few days later, only this time, I decided to bring him to the present moment and get an answer to my question. His eyes were darting around the room; I repeated the question. Someone came over and drew his attention there; I repeated the question as if it were brand new. At last, he gave me an answer. Is there a cycle of delivering a communication, receipt of it and duplication of the message? How do you know your communication is received? There needs to be an acknowledgment of it. The teacher is going to have to find something she and the student can agree upon, develop some affinity for one another in order to prepare the student to receive the communication. Then the communication must be delivered in the correct tone, usually high tone. There can be a two way cycle or one way cycle of communication, but these three things: affinity, agreement, and communication, must be in place. They must be in place because they lead to understanding.

To really learn communication, one must have the sequence of necessary steps. These steps are drilled and drilled to perfection. I use the sequence of steps from one of the fundamental communication courses taught at Applied Scholastics International. There are some basics that need to be in place for the student to get started. He must be in present time, and he must confront school and the subjects of study. That means being there comfortably! It forms the foundation of communication in school. It is not a given and must be taught. Getting to the school and being present, not only physically, but also mentally, is step number one. Being there comfortably without any reservations, in present time and ready to go to work, is where we want our students, if the learning is to stick. We have all experienced the excuses of why students cannot get themselves to school:

Learning Disabilities: The Myth

medical appointments, slept late, took care of younger siblings, skipped, my mother forgot to set the alarm, and you name it. They are avoiding school because they do not understand their purpose as a student, cannot confront their courses, and are most likely out of communication with their teachers, subjects and school in general. Many are unwilling and burned-out by the time they reach high school and are forced to come, if they come at all. All the significance of their courses, coupled with the misunderstood words, leads to non-comprehension of subject matter. Once in school, they frequently are tardy to class or skip out of school altogether. Somewhere they have lost their self-determinism and self-respect about schooling. Often they are not in present time and have sunk into an apathetic condition about learning. They present their bodies but their minds are elsewhere, on last night's date or tomorrow's football game.

Why is this? Has Western education helped to create this apathetic attitude? For one thing, the student cannot confront the school, the building even, let alone the materials, texts, and teachers. This has been called "school phobia" or "depression" by some learned folks in the field of psychology and psychiatry, "truancy" by the administrators, "lazy" by the teachers, "sick" or "just being a teenager" by the parents. Everyone calls it something else, and none of it answers the question or resolves the problem. The student can and does, therefore, hide behind these excuses. No one has a workable plan, and the student sinks, because he is not required to confront his problems and find the answers.

Communication is the one thing that all mankind does, and so you would think that it would be a priority in our curriculum, but it is not. It is not even taught now or has it ever been in any school in which I have worked as a teacher or attended as a student. When I began examining what was wrong in our school and looking for ways to right the wrongs, I discovered that this single most important skill was lacking. It was lacking among students, parents, colleagues and staff, and I, too, was deficient. So, I searched until I found some answers, and a communication course I took began to provide them. I spent hours and hours in training on these communication drills until they were polished. And this was only the first step in a very basic course, but it worked. It worked so well that I began to apply this in my classroom with my students, about 20 minutes each time we met. The only sad thing is the students need it as a full year course, one period a day to truly master the first level. After that, they are going to demand more communication courses. So the number-one communication drill at the beginning of the school year is to have the students confront (be there comfortably) the school building, the classroom, and then their texts and materials. They do this by just looking without blinking or flinching or talking. If the group is composed of freshmen, we make a trip outside to confront the building, and in sequence: the classroom, course materials, textbooks, the LI aide, and the teacher. Finally, the students work in partners and begin with the first drill. Getting an answer to their question is the fourth drill, for instance, but it takes some time to get here. One student discovered that she could get answers to her algebra questions by using her communication cycle and repeating the question. The teacher had a habit of bird walking, or avoidance.

ADHD students suffer from communication problems, as do all students in my program to a lesser or greater degree. Lack of communication skills and bad control can cause a student to exhibit in-seat and out-of-seat behaviors, not listen, not follow directions, and to wander around the room. Communication drills can fix the problem. Jeffrey's mother was adamant about getting him on Ritalin because she had seen the wonders of it. I suggested that she give us the year and see how things go. Jeffrey was a student with excellent scores on the Terra Nova (system-wide tests) and never did belong in a special program. He was making failing grades because he would not do his homework or class work. It is what I dub the "Mommy Do It" syndrome. So I leaned on him a bit, but the deciding factor was the communication routines that we do daily. I knew that he would test out of the program this year, and the mother was determined that he would not, so she was going after the Ritalin. This year, he is no longer a blob like the character, Jabba the Hut, from *Return of the Jedi*, sitting, looking pleasant while someone else takes care of him. The communication drills changed all that. He is focused and doing his work, productive, and happy. Unfortunately, the family left before it was time to test him again. My hope is that they avoid the prescription drugs.

Learning Disabilities: The Myth

    Christa is a prime example of one who was out of communication with her environment and her body. She could not confront her course work, especially math, her classmates, and least of all herself. Putting her on a gradient of learning and using word-clearing procedures and a step-by-plugging-away-step process made the difference for her. Christa did not want to be with others; it was too painful. She created a problem for the entire class by not bathing for days. The stench would get so bad that other students, especially the conduct disorders, began to torment her outside of my class and in other classes, as well as on the bus. A visit to the nurse did not make the situation any better nor did numerous calls to her mother or calls to her father, a colleague at another school who is divorced from the mother. The father is rather a milquetoast individual who busies himself with his own life in the theater, and the German mother needs institutionalization. When Christa left the classroom each day, the entire room stunk, and keeping the windows open in the dead of winter did not help clear the foul odor or increase her prestige among her peers.

    What did work, and worked extremely well, was getting Christa to define the word hygiene. We did this in a session together after school. She looked up hygiene, defined the word, and then made many sentences with all the different definitions. If there were misunderstood words within each definition, she got those defined and understood. Next, she read over the synonyms, word usages, and word derivations, until these were understood. Within hygiene, she found sanitary as a misunderstood term, and repeated the same procedure. Then she cleared the word stench. That was the word I was hoping she would run across. After clearing stench, she illustrated this with a character from one of her video games and called it fly honey. I asked her to describe for me how she bathed. She laughed and said this was embarrassing but proceeded to tell me precisely how her mother runs the water for her (she's sixteen years old, mind you) and how she sits in the water. Her father stated that generally she gets the first cycle of the water that is shared by one other family member in order to economize. (Now, I imagine his salary is right about what mine is, and there is no shortage of water.) Then, when her mother allows, she shampoos her very long hair while sitting in the tub. When I asked why she did not use the sink, she stated if she bent over she got headaches. So she sits, soaks in recycled lukewarm water, and then gets out and towels off. End of bath!

Now I said, "Christa, I will show you how I bathe myself." She laughed and said okay. As I proceeded on my body from top to bottom, she said, "This is really getting embarrassing!" and I replied, "It's going to get better," as I showed her how I washed my behind. By then, we were both laughing hysterically. I asked, "Christa, what do you use to bathe yourself?" When she gave me a blank stare, I asked if she would like to use what I did, and she replied she did, only she preferred that I not get her anything pink. At our next session, I presented her with a blue mitt and good-smelling liquid soap. Following this session of word clearing and confronting her problem, she only needed one additional reminder and that was over a year ago. She has remained clean!

Jerry proudly announced, "Cheese!" and the entire class rang with laughter. I was seated in the back of the classroom being as unobtrusive as possible and discreetly making notes on Jerry's behavior and responses. His teacher had suspected some type of learning problem and asked if I would have a look. It was Valentine's Day, and the students were playing a word game. The students were going through the alphabet in turn and answering the question with their letter: "What would you send your sweetheart?" Jerry's letter was C. He was totally unaware of his environment and what question had been asked; he did know that he had to do something with letters and he had to make a word with the letter C. I estimated that his problem was language (communication), and it was later proven to be so.

Sasha was an eager student right from the beginning, not only for academics and Study Technology, but also for communication. She began clearing up her misunderstood words the minute she understood that this could be the basis of her language and learning problems. After two years in my reading program, she was ready to tackle senior English. She kept herself busy defining her misunderstood words and soon was using words like oxymoron with understanding. Her English teacher was astounded.

When Penny joined my class, her teachers said she was sleeping, "daydreaming", or doodling in class and, of course, not completing her work. Shortly after joining my class, she put her head down on the table and covered her head. I said, "Sit up, Penny!" She did but was nearly in tears. We left promptly for my office, and I questioned her about sleeping and asked her if she felt bad. She replied, "My life is ruined!" We took my box of colored blocks out and my sketchpad. I let her talk and I listened, assuring her that this was confidential. She went on to tell me that her dog in the U.S. had died. I asked her to tell me about the dog. She replied, "My dog was found by my grandfather and it died. He had been abused." She was that dog, I was sure. I showed her with my demonstration kit about the communication cycle, and we worked from there.

Penny had many problems besides academic such as crying jags, sleeping in class, poor hygiene, and not completing work, though she was very capable. She had been placed in my program some months ago. During two private sessions I was able to bring her up tone and get her to produce and do much better, although it did not entirely fix the problem. Generally, Penny was very resistant to anyone helping her at all, or "looking over her shoulder," as she called it. I agreed with her because she does know how to do her work when she is in present time, so I let her be. Already I had strong suspicions of abuse, physical or verbal or both. By the end of the year, she got better, following a session where she had a look at her life in Germany, but this was only the tip of the iceberg. Her mother had been deployed to Iraq while Penny and her younger siblings stayed back with the father who had recently retired from the military.

Here's the part that was a shocker to me. Penny had declined drastically in her behavior and attitude toward school over the summer, and when she arrived in late August, it was like starting all over again. She would have temper tantrums, cry, become uncooperative, resistant, and began sleeping in class again. She would not do her work and was utterly failing. She was miserable and, I thought, suicidal. One day, she got out of control in the classroom, totally unprovoked, so I allowed her to call her father and sent her to the nurse to get another opinion. She wanted out of my class for no reason, but I agreed, knowing that this was not the true story.

When her father arrived, I suggested to both that she could be self-determined about my class. Though the father was not willing, he gave the impression that it might be okay for her to drop out of the program. When given a choice, she became determined to stay.

After an interval of the weekend, Penny came to me and immediately requested that I meet with her privately. "I have some secrets," she said. I assured her that they would remain so. She was distraught and appeared really depressed. What could I do? What I would not do would be to send her to our psychologist; this would be sentencing her to a DSM diagnosis without a workable plan, and drugs, most likely. Instead, I got a pad of paper and my blocks, and we went to my office. She talked and I listened. I used my demo kit again; she defined her problem and made sketches. She is quite a good artist and enjoys sketching, so this was a good avenue for her to express herself. We looked at her sketches together as she sketched her family and the problem. I had her identify where the communication problem was. She described it precisely. She defined words and I listened. Her tone came way up and I thought this incident was finished.

Well, in a couple of days, she was back asking to speak to me about an incident that had occurred that evening. I thought, *What am I going to do this time to help?* Looking at the communication cycle was not enough! We looked at the communication break one more time, and she identified where the problem was. So she described her problem again as she set the scene with the blocks. She had experienced a really horrible incident with her parents that included cursing, tears, and threats. She told them she hated them because of their huge invasion of her privacy. She talked about physical abuse from her mother, who she described as unfeeling and uncaring. I suspected sex abuse from the father, which causes the abuse from the mother. She hated them both, she said, and wanted to leave home; she was threatening suicide. She said her mother accused her of wanting to take her place, and that her father did not defend her or understand her. She said that she had even gone on the Internet to a chat room to get some advice. I listened and acknowledged but never evaluated or told her what to think. What to do? I asked her to "Go back over the incident; see if you can remember anything else." She did, again and

Learning Disabilities: The Myth

again and again, until this huge, emotional charge was lifted. I asked her what she saw, heard, and felt and to describe all her perceptions. She looked away from me as she recalled her pictures. "Uh-huh, alright, okay, good," I would acknowledge at appropriate intervals. (Fortunately, I had the students in my classroom well trained, and they knew what to do without me or else I never could have gone away with another student across the hall and into a private office. Also, my aide could run intervention, if necessary.)

Eventually, she found a solution on her own, without a hint of suggestion on my part or any evaluative statement. The charge dropped off this horrific incident and she was free of it. It was magic! She had gone down, down, down and then up, up, up in tone all in about forty-five minutes. Oh yes, I remembered I needed to bring her to present time (thankfully) by having her find something pleasant in the room. She came back to the classroom and worked better than she had worked all year long. And she has maintained this level for months now and periodically smiles at me. (Just think if I had sent her to the nurse or psychologist; there is a very good chance that she would be on psychiatric drugs right now, I have no doubt about it.)

Three quarters later, Penny is still holding her own, has friends and a special male friend that she delighted in telling the class about during our sharing of success stories. More recently, her physics teacher wrote that she had an A with a comment: "Do you know how hard it is to get an A in my class?" I printed this off and gave it to Penny to share with her father who called here a 'Retard' a while back. Her mother has now returned and the home front appears fairly stable at the moment. Penny nearly made the honor roll last quarter and vowed to this quarter. Although, she did slip with homework completion, she is in the process of catching everything up as she works furiously to meet the end of quarter deadline. Regardless, Penny is on the way up!

Establishing Control

Last year I encountered the most difficult group of freshmen that I had ever experienced in all my years of teaching. They were not in present time, never had the correct materials for study, and were constantly talking, regardless of requests to stop. Like a stuck record, I found myself repeating, "Stop talking, get in your seat, get your materials. What *was* your homework? Not here. I see." They were somewhere else in the galaxy but not in my classroom, and no amount of entreaties to join the lesson made any difference. A couple were willing, that was clear, if only they knew how. *Whoa! What is the matter here?* I said to myself. This feels like my first day ever in a classroom. I have to get in control here.

My first teaching job was at a school called Green Acres, a pilot school for the severely emotionally impaired. I was hired at the county level just in time to meet the students the next day. I met with the principal; he gave me a brief orientation and showed me my room. I was literally thrown into the classroom without materials or a mentor or anything. The very next day, here came the students as I was rushing around trying to figure things out. Instinctively, I knew that I had to keep my students busy and look busy. That was what education valued then and that is what education values today. Keep 'em busy! So during my first day of class, I passed out history textbooks and told Dan, "Put away what you're reading and open your history book." Imagine my shock when he rolled his eyes back, completely stoned, and replied, "Lady, I'm reading my goddamn Bible!" I knew then and there that being a schoolteacher was no picnic, and that I had my work cut out for me. No one had bothered to tell me that these students were at all different levels of learning, and that this one in particular could not read at all, not to mention that he was high on dope. See, I was a certified teacher of the deaf, and landed this job because no one else wanted it. No one wanted this job because these were reportedly the toughest students in the county. The county needed a certified special education teacher, someone green enough to take this job. So I took the job and was placed on a provisional certificate and given the year to get the certification of the emotionally impaired. The first lessons I learned on my first day were that most of these students had reading problems and that they did not know their purpose as a student.

Some of these students were straight out of psychiatric institutions, many were on prescription drugs, and others were on probation from the local juvenile detention centers, and some of these were on street drugs. They were the rejects, the troublemakers from the local schools. Green Acres was an alternative school, and students were sentenced to serve anywhere from three months to a year there. They were assigned to one of two teams at the rear of the school. On our wing, one team applied behavior management, the other team (mine) applied counseling. The other wing at the front of the school had the serious students with multiple handicaps such as autism and students who could not exercise any self-control. One insane student on the front wing had already slugged the teacher in the face, breaking her jaw. The mother had hotly defended her son's action and said, "I already told you how to handle Jeremy." She used a cattle prod to control him! I was indeed grateful that I was spared that teaching assignment as my first.

The so-called counseling used by our team was undeniably a waste of time and quickly abandoned with team agreement; there was little planning, and students sat around and gabbed and enjoyed not having pressure to learn anything. Each teacher had an aide, and mine was a certified elementary teacher who wore red patent stiletto heels admired by a student with a severe foot fetish. It was at first amusing watching him watch her slender feet. Now, on the first day without prior warning, both of us had to manage physical education, she in her stiletto heels, and I in my stacked heels. We never had a break all day. These students could not be left for a minute by themselves, not for a bathroom break, not for lunch. We managed everything!

Point System

Very soon our team at Green Acres switched to behavior management and a point system to establish better control. The control we used was bad control, but it worked. We gave each student a colored card when they walked in the door each day—different day, different color—that had their name written on it and POINTS typed across the top. I had a hole puncher that I used, and I would walk up and down the aisles, intermittently punching holes in their cards if they were quiet and appeared to be doing something I had assigned. You could have heard a pin drop, had it not been for the click-clack of the hole puncher. I found out later that I was being observed through a two-way mirror by the principal and higher-ups from the county, and all were awed at this very good control and delighted that students were *busy*. To tell the truth, I knew that I was only keeping them from rioting, and their reward for the silence was a smoke break. It was a step up from the discipline used by the assistant principal, whose method was to bark orders and use physical force, if necessary. I recall he made one offender in the other wing stand facing a chalkboard with his nose in a circle for I do not know how long. Eventually, this assistant principal and I were at loggerheads, and I resigned.

Within three weeks, I was hired at another school; the principal called me because his wife, who was a counselor at the school I had just left, recommended me. Now that I had almost completed the emotionally impaired certificate, I needed a certificate in learning disabilities. Once again I would teach with a provisional, only this time my fellow special education teachers would hire me. This school had a very large population of special education students. It was located in a low socio-economic neighborhood where learning was not the number-one priority for these students or their families. Surviving was. The students I would be working with were in a resource model. What a mix it was of students with conduct disorders (behavior disorders), slow learners, and learning disabilities. The more severe LD and BD were in separate, self-contained classes.

Every Friday at this middle school, free time was granted to students who earned the necessary points. Those who did not were required to spend the time doing work. We swapped the duty among the team members, and every one of us hated it when it was our time to monitor free time. The *good guys* got to eat candy, popcorn, and choose an activity such as watching films, playing games, or talking. It could get loud and almost out of hand sometimes. The principal, Mr. Livvy, loved to come by for a visit on Free Friday and play games with the students. He seemed to appreciate our spirited team. The *bad guys* had to complete unfinished homework or do additional assignments. One Friday when it was my turn to keep the workers, I noticed that Cal, a puffy, red-faced kid, with long shaggy unkempt hair, was not accounted for when I called roll. Cal was a tough one to handle, often becoming enraged at the slightest provocation, and I was not looking forward to hauling him into my class. As quickly as I could I hurried over to one of my colleagues to try and locate him. When I questioned him about Cal's whereabouts, my colleague said, "Cal told Mr. Livvy to kiss his ass and ran out." I asked, "Why?" He replied, "Mr. Livvy asked him why he didn't get his points for free time."

Stamping out fires and trying to make sense of the paperwork and regulations were my next lessons as I became the long-term substitute. I could already see that the terminology had been created by a system that was totally out of control and had lost touch with its purpose, if it ever defined one in the first place. To teach these students by the book was a waste of time, not to mention impossibility, so I began to apply what worked and what seemed to be natural. It was only later that I found out why the technology I employed worked, enabling me to refine it. This was a diverse and fun team of teachers, fully supported by the principal, who wanted us to teach these students and bring them up to literacy if only we could find the way. We were a team in every sense of the word and our control improved, along with student learning. We used points, a reward and denial system, and about anything else that would get students to behave and learn. We were on the way but had not arrived. Eventually, I moved away from this great team to set up a program for high school deaf and hearing-impaired students in a town in the middle of the state. Never again would I experience the kind of teamwork we had.

At this next school, no point system was needed. I faced different challenges though and was completely alone. I had five students, all profoundly deaf. I was told that all my students were oral; this was a great relief to me, because the world talks. Having a student use sign language in a high school, where no one else but the teacher knew it, would definitely be a problem. These students were fun, all motivated to learn and good students. These were the best students

I have ever encountered. They had to be the best; otherwise, they never would have made it this far in a public school.

Glenda, a senior, was a lovely young woman with dark hair and huge brown eyes that could almost talk. Her speech was so good that she sounded like a foreigner that spoke English and retained a slight accent. She planned to go to Gallaudet College, the college for the deaf and hearing impaired in Washington, DC. Suzon was an excellent student, tenth grader, who participated in everything in school and was able to take all regular classes without any additional help. In contrast to Glenda, she could be a bit defensive and somewhat haughty. Both girls always made the honor roll. Suzon planned to go to college and study teaching. Robby was a fun-loving guy and very much interested in the social scene at school. He was outstanding in speech reading and could read someone from the side and at a distance. This allowed him to get into everyone's business; he was like a vacuum cleaner sucking up the gossip. No secrets from him! This repetition of gossip aided his language skills enormously though. He wanted to be a beautician and never tired of commenting that my hair needed his expertise. Eventually, I set up a practical experience for him at the county vocational school where he fit right in. Dan and Jack were on the football team and very popular. Dan had many friends and was a big man around the campus because he was the quarterback on the winning football team. He would not always wear his hearing aid and would not always do his homework, but he would do enough to get by in his classes. His family would support him with any vocation that he chose.

My challenge was working with Jack. He was the only son of one of the wealthiest families in the county. They were a most supportive family and did everything they could for their son. They wanted more than anything for him to speak and appear normal and had sent him to all the best oral schools available. Nothing worked; he could not learn to speech read. As a result, he never learned straight language. He was totally isolated! I had to teach him everything but Physical Ed. He was a great mathematician and Algebra was a breeze for him, thankfully. His lack of language began to present real big problems before long when he began to want to be with the opposite sex. I did some research about schools and, finally, I convinced his family that he should go to the Gallaudet Model School for high school students, also in Washington, DC. There he would learn total communication which would include sign language so that he could communicate and have friends. I was relieved that I had made a good plan for Jack before I left at the end of the school year. Later, I did hear from the counselor that Jack's family had followed through with Gallaudet Model School and that Jack was doing very well.

I returned to my previous county and took a job in another middle school. Here I was assigned a class of severely learning disabled students. I quickly implemented a point system again. I knew that the point system was working when Cassie walked out of the classroom in a huff. I heard her utter under her breath, "Bitch," when she was not awarded her points. Unfortunately, she knew that I had heard her, so we both went to the office, otherwise, I would have ignored the comment. In the office, we called her mother, and I had her repeat what she had just said to me. "Called her a bitch," Cassie said. Her mother, a big, burly woman who was a butcher at the local grocery store and also drove one of the county school busses, said, "I'll be right over." Now, I did not want to wait around to witness the abuse that was about to be heaped on this girl. I did know that she would probably threaten her and beat her within an inch of her life. I felt bad about that for a long time. This was the same school where a mother had come to the school when summoned, walked right into the social studies classroom, and called her son to the front of the classroom. Before the dazed teacher could halt her, she commanded him, "Drop your pants!" He did, and she proceeded to flail the daylights out of him with a belt in full public view. His offense had been that he "mooned" the class the day before. (He had dropped his pants, bent over, and showed his rear amidst the uproarious laughter of his classmates and the chagrin of his teacher, who walked in at the tail end of this episode.) The teacher never had any more trouble with this boy acting up.

I had one more experience with keeping points as a reward system before I gave them up entirely. I was teaching regular students in a fifth-grade classroom and experimenting with cooperative learning groups. I divided the class into six different teams for cooperative learning activities. I kept two big colorful charts for points, one with team names and one with individual names. I was proud that I could get the students to arrange their desks into groups of six with their teams in less than two minutes with complete silence. Points were awarded for speed and silence. The students decided on team names such as the Blue Dolphins, the Demons, and so on. (One mother demanded that the team change the name from Demons to something else due to her religious beliefs. So I said her daughter could choose another team or work alone, but the team names would remain.) It was a busy year, one where I exercised good control over my teaching. We did an ecology project that year that I took across the curriculum and teamed with a third-grade teacher for writing projects, math projects with the New Math Standards, field trips, and computer projects. I was trying to be as innovative as I could and put in long hours to get it all accomplished, as do most elementary schoolteachers.

One day I got a call from a disgruntled father of one of my students, demanding more points be awarded to his daughter's team. He had already called the principal complaining that his daughter's team did not get all their points that they were supposed to, and so and so's team got too many points. Can you imagine! I could not figure this out, so I said, in controlled sarcasm, "How many points would you and your daughter like?" He told me and I said, "Alright, done. Is there anything else?" He replied rather startled, "No." I announced to the class the next day that this was the end of the point system.

Help Is Possible

I have come a long way since my first years in the classroom; I never need points anymore to establish and keep good control. Today, I get good control by recognizing that the student is a spiritual being. He, therefore, must be self-determined and at cause over his learning and behavior. It is very rare that I have ever needed to remove a student from my classroom even temporarily; though I have pulled a few aside to talk to them privately. This usually follows an upset from home or in another class that carries over to my class. Nearly every time, we resolve the problem. I do anticipate problems and isolate students within the classroom as needed.

Learning Disabilities: The Myth

The year I had the *freshmen from hell* must have been a bad year astrologically. Not only was I affected in my classroom but the entire school felt the challenge and energy drain. It was not that they were so bad in general but they never listened, never stopped talking, and challenged your every utterance. They never had materials, never knew or cared what assignments were given, and certainly were not about to waste their precious time on doing homework. They were rude, unprepared, off-task, and mean to each other. One student I'll call Kyle was an example of "hate-on-hold," and ready to explode. He could best be described as one who looked as though he could bring in an automatic rifle and mow me down along with his classmates, and anyone else who looked at him wrong. One student, Chandra, was a hellcat, glaring at me as if I had insulted her the minute I said, "Good morning." Another student, Sid, was fourteen going on six and constantly interrupted and made bids for attention. It was impossible to complete a sentence in his presence. Gary had his own world of Gothic symbols, Celtic jewelry, and tattoos. Oh yes, he bragged about having various tattoos on private parts of his anatomy. (I call this the genital stage.) Brigitte, while more capable and motivated than the rest, could not hear a word because she talked nonstop, and no amount of coaxing could get her to rest her jaws and give the rest of us some peace. Jeffrey sat like Jabba the Hut from *The Return of the Jedi*, waiting to be fed. He was incapable of lifting a pencil. Salina could not read but made up for it by constant chatter with Brigitte and Chandra. These are examples of the makeup of my charming group of ninth-graders on the first day of school. What to do? I wanted to leave.

I had some challenges in my other classes too, but not of this magnitude. I had two non-readers, including an English as a second language student, plus three more with severe deficits in reading. I had to think pretty hard about how I would bring them up the bridge of learning. This group was worse than last year's crop, and last year I had wanted to leave for sure. Of course, there are always exceptions to the rule, and within this hodgepodge of students with low skills and devil-may-care attitude were two students, also with low skills, who were motivated to learn and generally knew what was going on in the other classrooms. (They are your salvation, so cultivate their successes and use them to help.)

The year before, the freshmen were just downright mean, I mean *mean*, but easier to control in the classroom. They had no definition for ethics as a group. Most were stealing, lying, fighting, swearing, and all failing or near-failing with few exceptions. These poisoned the good students, as is often the case. What a challenge that had been. The difference when compared to this current group was that I could get them to be quiet, although they were not really hearing me. I had non-readers as well and students who had had a history of Fs and Ds and hated school. Here is an example. During the first lesson in reviewing for world cultures, when told to get out their *Current Issues* book, I was boldly told in no uncertain terms by Joe, "These ain't fucking current issues!" Immediately, I had to stop whatever review I had in mind and deal with this behavior. First, I acknowledged that they were not current issues, then we talked about consequences for his lack of control. Later on, his reading deficit would show up. And this is what set him off, I am sure, the fear of reading aloud.

Once you have looked over your students and gotten some idea of the help that is needed for each one, have them establish that help *is* possible. I got this idea from a seminar that I observed in St. Louis, Missouri. You can do this by a series of drills. Have the students get in pairs and think about a time that they received help. Each student tells his example to his partner and then the partner tells about his example. Next, they come up with a time when they helped someone. Again, they switch. Now they think of a time when they observed someone helping another. Swap stories again. Finally, they find an example of a time they helped themselves. Swap stories. When this drill is completed, ask them if they believe that help is possible. Acknowledge them for this discovery. You cannot get to first base unless they believe that they can be helped.

Purpose

Establishing good control and routines is the basic ingredient for a successful year. We always start the first class of the school year by defining the purpose for coming to school. Why study or

Learning Disabilities: The Myth

bother at all? They tell the purpose, but first we define purpose by looking in a good student dictionary. Students do not really know what their purpose is in coming to school. No one ever explained it. It was just expected that they would know it. Therefore, during the first day or so of school each year, the students help define their purpose as a student. This becomes the first routine, finding out what a word really means, no guessing, and selecting the correct definition among those listed that fits. The teacher does not give it to them. After some questioning and brainstorming, I write their ideas all over the board, and they define their purpose, which is study which leads to good grades and graduation, future employment, or more schooling. They use the dictionary to verify their understanding of the word and define other words within the definition, if necessary. It is important that we have agreement here, because it lays the cornerstone for their being at school in the first place.

Kyle said, "You go and get good grades so you can go to college. Then you can get a good job."

I ask, "Why?"

This leads one to say, "So we can afford things!"

Another adds, "To eat, have a car and house."

Again, I ask, "Why?"

Liza says, "We want to be comfortable."

"Why?"

Jeremy says, "To survive!"

"Thank you!"

I ask, "How do you want to survive?" They think this over a minute.

One said, "Good," and another replied, "Be happy." All noble reasons. "Well, okay," I say. "We will take up this happiness idea on another day."

Now that we have established our purpose for being in the class and coming to school at all, we talk about the student hat and teacher hat. We talk about hats as being the profession one has over a lifetime, and some have many. In the cemeteries of Istanbul, the big hats on the tombstones represent the various professions of those buried there. So they look this idea over and decide that the student's hat must be to study and apply this knowledge. Then we discuss the teacher's hat, which they decide is to help them achieve their purpose.

Student Hat

I explain that each of us wears many different hats: teacher, student, son, daughter, parent, and so forth. These hats define our roles. No one ever explained what being a student really meant. What was it all about, the role and purpose? Using the dictionary, my ninth-graders defined student, and within student they found the word study, and within that knowledge, and within that know.

"Wow! Could we say that "to know something" is an important reason for coming to school?" I asked. "What do we do with this information when we know it?" I continued.

"You do something," said Liza.

"Like what?"

Each student is given an opportunity to tell what he could know and what he could do with this knowing. This understanding the role of student was another big step in being in the present moment. So the students found that their purpose was to know, to observe and find out things and then apply. These two exercises helped the students in becoming self-determined on their purpose and role.

Teacher Hat

Together we look up the definition of teacher. "One who imparts knowledge or skill or causes to learn by example or experience" is the definition given in the *Second College Edition: American Heritage Dictionary,* Houghton Mifflin Co., 1991. The teacher's role is to help the student distinguish between what is true and what is false. The student then can make his own conclusions so that he can then apply the data. It is important to get across the idea of application.

Control

Once we are in agreement on our roles and purpose, we can move into the area of control. In order to achieve our purpose, good control must be established, agreed to, and maintained. This is one of the most important things you can do when you begin the year; so

Learning Disabilities: The Myth

try to establish it on the very first day with a new group of students. Now I had always considered that I established control very easily and things just fell into place, but over time I found out a better way to establish control. I found out that sometimes I was employing bad control.

Have your boundaries and classroom rules in mind beforehand, but allow the students to participate in establishing those that affect them. Make sure that all understand and that you are proceeding in an up-tone fashion, firm but fair. The first day, establish routines and organize the classroom with the students' input. The hardcore behavior problems surface at once, so do not waste any time bringing them in line. Set the limits and stick with them. Boom! The first time they step over that boundary, haul them back in immediately. Be very firm. Simplify what it is that you expect all students to do and have them do it. Call them on it every single time it is not done. I say something like, "Let's talk about what it is we need to do in this class to achieve our purpose as a student."

We discuss what no control might look like in the classroom. Granted, some of these students have never had control at all and this is sickness itself. With no control, they can see that nobody could learn. Next, we look at bad control. Bad control would be punishment for their overt actions against each other and the environment, e.g., throwing an acting-out student out of the classroom or sending him to the principal. They get the idea, so now we need to decide how to set good control. They agree that the teacher has the right to exercise good control because it is part of her hat to help them achieve their purpose.

The students contribute to ways in which we can establish a good learning climate. I allow them to write all over the chalk board their ideas about ways to organize and manage the class. The students define the word control, and then we talk about no control, bad control, and good control. Next, the students look up the word control, and we take the appropriate definition: to exercise authority, influence. (Be sure you do not have dinky dictionaries.) Then when they are finished, say something like, "Well, these sure are a lot of rules. Do you think that we might cut these down a bit?" They are very surprised when you say, "I think we can shorten this list. What do you think?" They are really happy to cut down on so many rules. Then you are back in charge, yet you have given them a choice, and they can follow these rules more easily because they are self-determined. I congratulate them on their insight and contributions. Next, we put all these ideas under four general headings that become four rules for the class. I tell them, "I hate rules! Let's put down something that we can believe in, something that is real for us, and call these precepts for living a better life." We do; it is simple and it is always the same: I explain that it is like the Golden Rule, "Do unto others as you would have them do unto you" in the classroom, and it works every time. I pull out my laminated list from previous years, and they are amazed. It is what we just agreed to and had written on the board.

I will:
- Cooperate with the teacher and my peers.
- Try to complete my homework and class work.
- Bring my materials to class.
- Stay on task.

Once you have put good control in and keep it in, your life will be so much easier. By the end of the year, you wonder if they are going to ever act up again. You hope not, but it is so peaceful, it is almost dull. Students are working with a purpose, and following good routine and order, and learning. By second quarter, 70 percent are on the honor roll. These are happy students, almost like contented cows. Every now and then, one student may hang on to old, disruptive, nonproductive patterns, bad lessons learned well, but you can always trace it to some upset at home or elsewhere, never in your classroom. By now you have reduced your troublemakers to one or two. Handle them swiftly but fairly.

Students who suffer from no control are really sick and act up at every chance they get, in one way or another. Some have been accustomed to responding to only bad control and will push the limits. Do not waiver in your reserve to put discipline in by helping them wear their student hat properly. They want and need control and need someone to be in charge. It is natural. They will respect

Learning Disabilities: The Myth

you for it. When you give a command, put your intention into it and know that they will keep it. One day I went down to the Science 9 class to get my aide and the minute I looked in, the male science teacher came hurrying over to me to report the disruptive behavior of one of my students. Then the aide who was in that class, primarily to assist this boy, reported on him. Michael was dismantling the lab experiments, mishandling equipment, talking, laughing and making rude comments. The teacher was afraid someone would get injured. The discipline plan was not working, apparently. I stepped in, gave the student a command with full intention, "Get your things and come with me, Michael. Now!" He got up, got his materials and backpack together, and followed me down to my classroom without a word. "You sit over there," I directed him, and pointed to the table. He sat down and did not move. After about twenty minutes, he asked, "May I read?" I replied, "Yes." He spent the next hour in isolation reading, sitting with his back to me. If I had not put my intention into the command, he probably would not have followed me. That was an example of good control but other-directed. What we want, eventually, is control, self-directed. This comes when Michael has self-determinism and is interested in his own progress.

<u>Acknowledgment</u>

Be sure to acknowledge students in conversation by modeling the training routines that are to come. I acknowledge their presence; they acknowledge mine. You have to train them that you are there; this gets them into present time. I acknowledge their responses. This carries over to acknowledging work. This will save you a lot of grief later on. You are establishing a climate of all business. And school is their business for the next nine months. This cures the attitude of sloppy permissiveness that prevails throughout many classes, and homes and schools in general. I tell my unruly ninth-graders, which includes a lot of conduct disorders on the very first day, "You don't do less in this class; you have to do more because you are behind." They may groan, but they get the picture. After getting their attention, I then explain the routines of the class.

Communication

Communication skills are vital for anyone, and in order to communicate, we must learn how to do it effectively. Communication is the one thing that is common to all human beings on the planet. Everyone talks about communication, but it never was defined adequately, and few were trained, if any, to teach communication in school. Oh, we have courses like speech in school, but that is only a very small part of what communication is about, and the lessons stay right there in the classroom anyway. A simple definition of communication is an exchange of ideas across space, but that does not tell one how to communicate. The drills I learned from a course on communication are what I use throughout the year and are mentioned in a previous chapter. I use them because they work! Do not neglect teaching your students how to communicate once you have learned it yourself.

Interest

Two students who entered my reading program after the start of school were huge behavior problems and were giving me fits. They would not pay attention, were talking, thumping, doodling, looking off, doping off, sassing, and never had their materials. Generally, students are so grateful to have some reading help that I seldom experience such resistance. These students did not have the same training as other students I teach regularly when I establish class routines that include ethics, concepts of help and control, and communication. I skipped these steps and plowed ahead with the description of the program and purpose. I had largely ignored the subject of interest in all my classes, assuming that whether they were interested or not, they would survive better in school. I was wrong! Interest is connected to self-determinism and just surviving in reading is never enough.

After a couple of failed lessons, I thought, *Boy, what am I going to do to get these two to be present and do what it is that they are supposed to do?* They had begun to poison the atmosphere for the others. I already had the tools of study and knew that they worked, but it had always been a gradual application with my other students. Eventually, all my students fall into line when they realize that the

Learning Disabilities: The Myth

gradient for reading is appropriate, clearing up misunderstood words is beneficial, and mass assists understanding. But with Nathan and Monroe, I could never get past the introduction of what it was we would be doing together each day. I knew that I could establish good control, but I needed their agreement in order to get their interest. Also, they would have to agree that help was possible and learn that communication was necessary. Getting the ideas about help, control and communication to work would be easy enough because I knew some drills and was convinced that this data, when understood, helps students learn.

So the very next lesson when these two boys began their antics, I immediately stopped the lesson and said, "That's it for the reading lesson!" and turned on the lights because we were viewing a video together and working on some very basic decoding drills for spelling and reading. They had learned the wrong lessons, and we had to unlearn those by putting in the following four factors:

Help
Control
Communication
Interest

I told them that in order to proceed and make progress in this class we needed to learn the right lessons on how to be ready to learn. The students defined these concepts in order followed by examples that they generated. The procedure is the same that I follow for my other students and explained previously. We also brought in the roles of student and teacher and defined responsibility to tie into help and control. On my bulletin board at the time was a nice display of a teacher's hat, and a student's hat, with roles and responsibilities as defined by my other students. This helped them and magnified the importance of what we were doing. Although there was no time to do communication routines, we defined communication and discussed how one can communicate with people and the materials of study.

These sessions about the first three points took up the next two classes. The third class was a miracle! The interest was there because the students were becoming self-determined as we got *in* help, control and communication. I led the discussion always in an up-tone manner and this, in itself, brought them into better communication. I discovered that one student was extremely interested in science fiction, and I shared a science fiction story with them that led to the discussion of traveling at the speed of light. We drew diagrams on the board and discussed the concept of time. The other student had a crashing misunderstood on continent, and we pulled down the wall maps of the world and looked at the continents. Then I made a diagram on the board to show him where he was at that moment in time, space and continent. The interest flowed naturally now from the self-determinism of the students. Good control, along with affinity, communication, and agreement that help was possible, made all the difference. This all adds up to understanding. I have not had a single problem since!

Classroom Management
- Muster.
- Set goals for class.
- Establish purpose.
- Do communication drills.
- Ethics training is provided one time per week
- Begin individualized work or small group instruction.
- Students proceed at their own pace.
- Access is available to clay table and demo materials, computers, calculators, resource books, dictionaries, and earphones (software, computer usage, and calculators are closely monitored.)
- Discipline Plan - See posted student-generated goals.
  A standard that I maintain is no talking, gum chewing, eating, or drinking. Water is allowed if bottle is kept on the floor. Talking is allowed if teacher directed or students are working with partners.
- Mail box for student information—Each grade level has a mailbox in which daily and weekly feedback from teachers is placed.
- Binders are kept on my bookshelf beside my desk with teacher feedback information. This is for reference and lesson plans.

Learning Disabilities: The Myth

- Conferences are held as needed with students to check understanding.
- MU's (Misunderstood words are cleared daily; dictionaries are on the table.)
- Successes are posted.
  The school honor roll with names highlighted is posted. Good papers from other classes, extra curricular achievements such as sports are noted.
- Monthly calendar lists upcoming projects, tests, due dates.
- Yearly calendar is on board.
- Bulletin board is important.
  Simple, bright, cheerful with theme of some subject or concept.
  One of the two long chalkboards in my classroom is used to post announcements, the calendars, schedules, school rules, and general information.
- Seating is structured.
  Students sit at two to three long rectangular tables put together to accommodate both the teacher and the teacher assistant or aide to move from table to table. I prefer several round ones for grouping, if available.
- Consumable materials are placed in an area that maximizes access for all.
- Sufficient and good dictionaries are available, and use is encouraged.
- Students organize themselves immediately as they come in—backpacks off the table, materials out.
- Order and neatness in classroom is stressed.
  Students are required to leave the class in an orderly fashion with chair placed under the table or computer desk. Paper and materials are picked up, and any trash on floor put away.
- Set weekly individual conferences of 5-8 minutes per student.
- Conferences are held with teachers and parents as needed. Students are free to set a conference any time.

Communication with Parents and Faculty

I explain, "Your business becomes my business if there are behavior or academic problems." I tell them that teachers complete weekly information sheets or send me messages through e-mail. I remind them that phone calls and conferences with parents occur as needed with teachers and parents and the student. There is a lot of structure and the gradient is low and slow until the student becomes more responsible for his learning and behavior. As students proceed with success, the reins are loosened and most become more responsible by their second year. If not and they lose ground over the summer vacation, the reins are tightened again. Generally, it does not take them as long as in the beginning to recover their gains.

Resources for Teaching

Teaching keeps you on your toes and you never are prepared enough for what society delivers to the doorsteps of the school. And this crop of freshmen was the toughest I had ever faced anywhere. They were merely a reflection of what was happening throughout the school, around the country, and in Western society. The majority of the students at my school continue to make D's and F's, and nothing the faculty has tried seemed to work very well or for very long. The only way that I was able to stay in this school with this population was to do something about it. I sought and found some answers that would bring my students up tone and send them on their way. I took a course in Fundamentals of Instruction and brushed up on using Study Technology and Communication at Applied Scholastics International in St. Louis, Missouri. There, I reviewed the barriers to study and the remedies. As a result, before I attempt to teach a student, I have a look at the student's learning rate, check for the proper study gradient, and then check for any misunderstood words. The needed mass in the form of demo kits and clay table are made available. In addition, I insure that I have gotten the four factors of help, control, communication and interest in place with students before I ever begin any lesson. These are the foundation of our established routines.

At the same time I discovered how I could apply some workable technology in my classroom, I learned about ethics as it pertains to all of life. I realized that I could not get the technology to work without including the ethics lessons. In life, we have a responsibility for not only ourselves, but for our family, the group, mankind, our environment, the physical universe, and the spirit. Applying methods I learned from these courses, books and other reading materials, put me over the top with these students. For many of my students and for me, it was a chance for understanding life through study. L. Ron Hubbard's Study Technology not only supported what I was doing already, it helped me simplify my teaching and understand what I knew. This was the foundation of learning and explained the enormous success some of my students experienced as a result.

Teaching Spirits

We need to know to whom we are teaching, what and how we are teaching. We are teaching spirits not bodies or animals. Students are not stimulus-response robots. Spirits have infinite capacity for learning, improving their intelligence, behavior and lives. Students can be more than they are, when they are self-determined. Given the correct study tools, we can determine what to teach these students and how to go about it. We can help them to rise up from the mire of Western education. This does not mean we proceed without structure. We must maintain structure and be firm in our resolve to help these students up the gradient of responsibility. If we keep in mind then that we are teaching spirits, we can have a future and bring students to achieve more worthily than they have in the past.

Tips for Managing the Classroom

When I discovered L. Ron Hubbard's Study Technology and his writings on education, I was validated about a lot of things. My school was working with some of the toughest students in the system worldwide, and I shared a lot of those students. I was always seeking new and better ways to improve student learning, knowing that all students could learn and apply knowledge. With the correct technology, I knew I could teach the student to confront his learning deficits and become self-determined. He would be able to proceed on a gradient in any subject and apply what he understood. I was trying a lot of approaches, hit or miss, and some worked, but I was not sure why. Hubbard helped me understand why what I did worked and to improve my teaching enormously. His writings removed the clutter and unworkable plans that get mixed in with what we do in my field. It simplified and straightened out my thinking, and gave me the foundation that I needed: the three barriers to study with their remedies.

Prior to studying Hubbard's technology for teaching and learning, I was aware of these barriers, but my remedies were not consistent. Students did make some gains if their deficits were not too severe, as most students learn to get by in school because that is what is expected. My students, though, required Herculean efforts to come forward because they were so low on the ladder of learning and were spiraling downward every year. Therefore, I studied these barriers with their symptoms and committed them to memory, and used the simple remedies for students studying material that was under my control. I practiced this technology until I mastered my craft and had these barriers down pat. Although I was able to control these barriers in my reading classes, I had little control over the study gradient that our curriculum set forth for all students to achieve mastery in a particular course. So I did what I could but found this next to impossible to better students' learning, unless the school joined in and applied this technology.

In this chapter, I talk about the barriers to study, and use of demonstrations with clay and demo kits. My understanding and application are based on L. Ron Hubbard's *Basic Study Manual*

(1992) and communication drills from courses taught at Applied Scholastics International in Saint Louis, MO. The three barriers to study that Hubbard isolated in his research are the *absence of mass, too steep of a study gradient*, and *the misunderstood word*. Each barrier has distinct physiological and mental symptoms; each has a distinct remedy.

I realized that although teachers learn about "barriers to study" at one time or another, their remedies get all mixed in with covering material, the latest gimmick for motivation, and psychological philosophies. Too soon, they forget these simple laws that govern one's learning and that the reason for learning anything is to apply it. Teachers forget this most important lesson: students have to be *taught* how to study; students have to be *taught* how to learn. We tell them to study harder, work harder, do your homework because practice makes perfect. Practice does not make perfect if the mass is absent, or the gradient is too steep, or a misunderstood word has been bypassed. If any one of these barriers is present, the gate to learning is barred, and the student will not be able to apply because he has not understood. The end result is that misunderstood words get piled higher and deeper causing a student to become a glib learner and get A's, or commit acts (minor or major, including criminal) against the environment, become totally lost in stupidity, or drop out altogether.

The following are some of the things that I do in my classroom that have worked very effectively, and that allow me to get the study technology in, and address the student as a spiritual being:

Start
Begin on time and end on time if at all possible. This sets a very good example that time in the class is important and should be used for the purpose of study.

Acknowledge
I always greet each individual student as he enters the classroom and say goodbye as he exits. This lets the student know that I am present, and I acknowledge that he is as well. You would be amazed

to know how many do not even know you are there and have not figured out that they are either. So you have to begin where they are and get them in present time. At first, I get little response, but I continue to greet each one cheerfully. Students can be trained to say good morning and acknowledge your presence.

I once had a student in a self-contained classroom for students with severe learning disabilities who was painfully shy (see chapter on reading) and really could not greet me. Her greeting eventually came as a soft and barely audible response accompanied by a noticeable smile. To check to see if my acknowledgment had made any difference, I withheld it one day as she was leaving, and she lingered at the door. I felt like a dog as she hung her head and left, and I never withheld it again. Finally, acknowledgment sticks and the student begins to respond, and eventually will greet first. It carries over to other areas. You could consider it a drill, but that is how it is learned, and it must be delivered in an up-tone communication line for it to become natural and second nature. After training the student to respond and initiate a greeting, I fade to see if there will be a response. Sometimes there is none, so I start again. This continues over the course of a quarter, and I fade again. More students greet me than before and sometimes come in the door with a cheerful "Good morning!" or "Good afternoon!" Eventually, I explain to them that I do not always feel terrific, but I can overcome this by making myself go up-tone. They get it.

<u>Beginning of Class</u>

When everyone has gotten to his seat, taken out materials including a dictionary, and put away backpacks, I go to the front of the classroom. I begin each class by mustering students in an upbeat (high-toned) manner and acknowledge each student as he answers the roll. If the class seems sort of drowsy and not very alert, I get them into present time with a communication drill. They respond to a few commands such as "Look at the ceiling" or "Look at the floor," "Stamp your feet three times," and "Touch the table."

Ethics

Ethics is defined as a principle of right or good conduct in the *Second College Edition: The American Heritage Dictionary,* c. 1991. Ethics must be present for any teaching technology to work. Ethics is doing what is the greatest good for the greatest number of people in relation to others and their environment. I use L. Ron Hubbard's *The Way to Happiness,* which has twenty-one precepts. It is a guide to better living, and I take up one precept a week. The students listen as I read, they define unknown words, and then we discuss the precept. These twenty-one precepts are read throughout the year, one a week, and then are compiled for a very attractive bulletin board as a summary.

When the precepts are completed and posted, we begin a discussion of human rights. I have some pamphlets and booklets that I use. It occurred to me that if we began teaching students at around the third grade about human rights and government, by high school they would be taking more responsibility in government. They would take responsibility, because by twelfth grade, when government is usually offered, they would understand the terms and have a clear idea of the inner workings of our government.

Although these discussions are limited to about ten or fifteen minutes per class period one time a week, it brings the awareness of the student up to a high level and increases his ability to look and take some responsibility for himself, the group, and his fellow man.

Set Goals for Day

Next, students set their goals for the day. Each one individually states what he plans to work on, and I write it on the chalkboard. For the more junior students (ninth grade in my current school) and those still in training, so to speak, I use teacher feedback and set the goals with them.

Start Work

Students start work as soon as the communication drills are completed. Students are prepared and ready to go to work. Not a minute is used for socializing.

End of Class

I go to the front of the class, and we go around the room to talk about our wins, our successes. If they cannot come up with one, I supply a personal one or one that I know about one of my students in another class. Also, I send out an e-mail periodically to my colleagues and ask them to e-mail me any wins students may have had. These are shared at the beginning of the class. Not all are academic wins; some are personal victories like Jack, who said, "I'm the third-best man on our tennis team." Actually, there were only three males all together, I learned. Nevertheless, the coach stated that this was indeed a big win for him, having the confidence to join the tennis team in the first place and working with the group.

Brandi shared that she received the highest grade on a test in all the English 10 classes, including the honor's classes. This was without any modifications, and her so-called deficit is in reading and language arts. I share that Alice in my ninth-grade class had the highest grade in all the Algebra I classes of a certain teacher. She supposedly has reading and language arts difficulties. Another student shares that she was instrumental in helping her volleyball team win a victory. Walter states that he just aced a chemistry test and has brought up his grade in Advanced Algebra.

Classroom Appearance

Keep the classroom neat and orderly. Students have a responsibility to help maintain a good atmosphere in the classroom as well as the materials, books, and equipment. Teach it and require it. I have found that students will take pride in a classroom if well organized and managed. They have access to materials but must request permission to use calculators, extra textbooks, and computers. These items are controlled for good reason but are always available. Supply materials are kept in a designated area, and students use them as needed.

Students are required to put their chairs under the table as they prepare for departure for their next class; I allow one minute only. The more time you give them, the more they will waste, and behavior problems may erupt. Structure is what they need, and it is tight. They will respect the property of the room and that of yours and others, if it is a standard and taught. Mutual respect and calmness ensue in an uncluttered and orderly classroom.

<u>Responsibility</u>

Regular-class teachers are always saying it is the student's responsibility to know the assignments, do them, and ask questions. Ms Bailey often refuses to give me information about students' assignments because "They need to be responsible!" That's right, they do, I tell her, but telling them to be responsible does not solve the problem. They do not necessarily demonstrate it automatically; in fact, they rarely do. Responsibility must be taught, and it must be taught on a gradient.

There are many different areas of responsibility for each individual such as self, family, group, the planet, animals and plants, and the spirit. Begin by helping the students look up the definition of responsibility and explain how the lack of it impacts their learning and lives. Give concrete examples and have the students give examples. Have them restate the definition until they can see what it is and get ownership of it. Have them demonstrate it with blocks or clay or role-play. Acknowledge them when they do show responsibility. I use examples as we work through the precepts during ethics training.

A big project that I do with students around Christmas time some years is to organize a banquet to teach students group responsibility. All agree to participate fully or not to attend at all. It becomes a very exciting experience for all and very rewarding in the end. For a few, this is the first sit-down dinner ever, and for one, it was the first home-cooked meal she could remember. "We cook all our meals in the microwave," she said. We write a Christmas letter to invite our parents, faculty, and special guests such as leaders from the district and others that we want to impress. It takes about three weeks to organize. Parents are called and reminded to send the portion of the letter back with what they agree to prepare with their student. Then they are called as a reminder about three to four days before the banquet. The special education staff contributes food as well, and we supply the paper products, tablecloths, and decorations. The banquet will consist of only home-cooked foods including meats such as turkey, ham, and chicken, various vegetable dishes; desserts of all descriptions; breads; water, tea, and sodas. Parents and the students choose from two categories and agree to prepare for twenty people. I always cook a lot, including a turkey, vegetables, and desserts because cooking, especially Italian, is one of my passions, and the banquet gives me a chance to cook American food for a change. Students are trained on manners and the purpose of the banquet, and their participation and duties are reviewed several times.

Anyone who might experience a hardship with bringing food is encouraged to speak to me privately. Together we find another way for each to contribute. Generally, there is no problem with the students in the community where I teach. Once I did have a young eighteen-year-old mother, who was on a very limited budget, make some wonderful computer-generated placemats as her contribution.

On the day of the banquet, my room is set up like a banquet hall with white lace tablecloths covering the extra tables borrowed from the media center and with centerpieces and candles. Two long, rectangular tables are covered in white, sprinkled with a little fresh greenery and a few bright round red glass Christmas ornaments, and set up at the front of the room with all the delicious food. I always coordinate with the home economics department to use the kitchens the night before and the day of the banquet. This has never been a problem. A couple of volunteer parents along with my students assist with warming the food and bringing it to the room. The chilled drinks are brought in about fifteen minutes before the bell for lunch. Also, I coordinate with the staff and administration ahead of time to allow the students to attend the banquet during seminar. Teachers come during their regularly scheduled lunch, and a few students and one or two parents assist. The majority of students attend the banquet during their seminar, the period following regular lunch. Unfortunately, only students and families along with teachers and a few dignitaries are invited. This can be as many as sixty to seventy people eating during the two shifts.

Finally, the scene is set with soft Christmas music playing in the background, and the warmth and glow of lighted candles on the tables. The scent of spices in pumpkin and apple pies, candied yams and roast turkey stuffed with sausage dressing, wafts through the hallway and temps others to peek in the door and ask to be invited. Some beg for leftovers and are accommodated, if they are part of the cleanup crew. The coffee starts perking, a signal to bring in the chilled sodas. Large bottles of water and soda are placed on the tables. Napkins and real cutlery are placed at each seat. The banquet is ready to begin. Students come in dressed to the nines, especially the girls, though I never said this was a requirement. They decided! I am dressed comfortably.

Midway through the dining, special guests are introduced and students are recognized for their achievements. There are always a fairly good number on the honor roll by this time. All students participate in one way or another, and many demonstrate their talents in music and public speaking. Last year, two students were the top students in all the Algebra I classes. Best of all, my students behave with almost impeccable manners and really shine. Every time at the banquet's end, I am exhausted and swear never to do another one. Still, I revel in the afterglow of my students' successes, and that is what lingers until the next time.

Clay Table

I have found that having the students use clay to demonstrate their understanding of words and concepts is a marvelous way to comprehend a subject because it provides needed mass. I end my reading classes by having the students model the definitions of two to three new words in clay. These words are words that have not been understood by the student. This takes about twenty minutes, if one is efficient. Have the student look up the word in the dictionary and then model it. I use the exact procedures in Hubbard's *Basic Study Manual* for clearing a word and for the clay demonstrations. When a student has understood the term or concept, he can work it out in clay.

I keep the following items handy in a closet for a fast setup of the clay table: several meters of inexpensive oil cloth, good clay stored in plastic ice cream tubs or Rubber Maid boxes, scissors, stiff paper or index cards, pencils, pens in a jar, table knife for cutting, and a couple of dowels. They label each part of the clay model of the word with a piece of stiff paper such as a 3 x 5 card (the cardboard insert from a new shirt will do) and place the word itself face down. When they have completed the first word, they raise their hand, and I check it. If they have not understood the word, then I take them back to the definition to find if there is a misunderstood word within the definition itself. All of these words must be cleared. If this is done consistently, these students will learn, their vocabulary will increase, and their IQs will rise. It is so simple and easy to do. By the way, good student dictionaries are essential so that the student does not encounter chains of misunderstood words within a single definition.

Using Demonstration Kits

Make up several sets of demonstration kits and have them in the classroom available for student use. Encourage the students to make their own from various handy objects to use in their other classes. These demo kits could be small wooden blocks of various shapes and colors, paper clips, pens, pencils, plastic Unifix Cubes or whatever is handy. Store them in cardboard or plastic boxes. The Unifix Cubes store well in plastic baggies. Also, I keep a large plastic bowl of colored wooden blocks on each table in the classroom. In one corner, there is a supply center and a cabinet where students are allowed to take materials as needed. Other materials such as technical, hundred-dollar calculators are necessarily kept under lock and key and handed out with some accountability.

You will need to show the students how to use these demo kits, and with some practice, they can get the hang of it. It is not always convenient to use the clay for demonstrations. Many of the math programs have blocks; certainly the algebra classes have kits. However, these demo kits can be used to clear up concepts on anything, not only math. I find that when I have used the demonstration kits to clear up my own thinking on a concept, it stays. I can see how it is and how it is not. I also do demonstrations for students when they just don't get it.

The other day, Brigitte said, "I don't get this world history assignment."

"Alright," I said, "Let's have a look," as I pulled out my small demo box of colored blocks and began to line them up to demonstrate each point. The assignment could be broken down into four parts:

select, research, and compare two methods, plus solutions for a problem in your school or community. The assignment was loaded with words that she did not know. Once we sorted through the definitions and brought her to full understanding, she could figure out what was required. "Oh, I get it! This is going to be interesting," she said. She is using two study techniques to learn and increase her understanding: word clearing and supplying mass.

Discipline

Over the last four or five decades, we have become very sloppy and permissive in our classrooms and schools. While I am not advocating a return to verbal or physical abuse in any way, I am suggesting that we take a look at how slack we have become and tend to let it all hang out and excuse students for lack of compliance to standard discipline and procedures. Now we are scrambling to bring some order to our classes, but we have to contend with the parents who were graduates of our undisciplined schools.

One of the first things I tell students is that nothing is wrong with them. So I expect them to learn, do their work and get help. There is structure and predictable boundaries. Firmness and fairness work. I accept the students as they are and intend for them to correct their problems, learning, and behavior, and they rarely disappoint me. Once they can look at their learning problems, find and figure out their misunderstood words, they start to improve and progress.

My classroom is very structured, and an agreed upon standard by students and teacher is maintained. The four agreed upon precepts for good class behavior are posted. Students do not talk during class as a general rule, although there may be talk with the teacher or another student (learning partner), if necessary. No eating, chewing gum, or drinking (water, if kept in a bottle on the floor) is permitted. Students can step outside with water for a drink. Having a no eating, no drinking policy protects materials and classroom and promotes a businesslike atmosphere in general.

Some teachers allow music, but it is not always soft and not always instrumental. Some say it soothes and assists learning; I say it is distracting and interferes with concentration and remaining in the present moment. So, no music in my class, unless it is for a specific assignment or event.

I do not allow a student to say negative comments or invalidate any teacher, adult, or another student. It serves no useful purpose. Immediate action is taken for such acts. In fact, I do not permit it and do not listen to it, so it rarely has to be confronted. One cannot accomplish learning in a positive, upbeat manner if this type of talk creeps into the classroom and becomes a standard.

Communication Drills

Often communication is impaired along with perceptions in such a way that the student cannot hear clearly what is being said due to pain or fear or other upsets; he may not see clearly or smell keenly, taste or experience all the many perceptions. Students want to communicate; it is a natural desire. However, it is not natural to communicate effectively. Communication must be taught with precision. We have lost the art of communication, if we ever had it ourselves. Teach the definitions of evaluate and invalidate while you are at it. Add this to the communication cycle and proceed. For instance, one drill students have to learn is to confront his partner without being thrown off by his partner's *pushing his buttons*. This is a tough drill but a very important one and needs to be monitored carefully.

These communication routines can be accomplished in a few minutes of each class daily. To teach the student to be in class comfortably and to confront the materials of study, his teacher, and classmates works! Recently, Lori was considering changing to another class, and I said, "Alright, good." Then she startled me when she said, "Do they teach communication routines and ethics in the other classes?" I responded, "No." She said, "Well, I'm staying with you!"

The year I had my *freshmen from hell*, I began the communication routines in earnest and on a regular basis after mustering the class. One protested and said, "It's not polite to stare," and most gave me all kinds of grief about doing these routines. I held my ground and reminded them that it was their choice to take this class but that it was mine to decide how to best help them. That affirmation from me, delivered in a very strong positive manner was enough. Now when I ask the students to get their communication cycle in, they know what it means. They come to attention with complete attention on the speaker and have the intention to receive (or deliver) the communication, with proper body posture, looking the person who delivers (or receives) the communication right in the eyes. They remember to acknowledge receipt of the communication.

A side note: one of my students had an "eye contact" IEP goal, and this totally resolved her problem of always holding her head down and staring at her hands or looking away. It was not long before Patty was looking her partner right in the eye, acknowledging, and speaking.

Gradient Approach

Students must be on a gradient, clearing up misunderstood words. The gradient approach should be used for everything. For example, Michael could not accept responsibility for his homework, getting his materials to class, or telling the truth. He has had many breaks on learning and lost his self-determinism about school a long time ago. His biology teacher had no patience for this because he was constantly off-task and not doing his work. She had difficulty understanding that each small step forward is a step in the right direction. Responsibility like everything else is on a gradient, also. Too steep a gradient for anyone impairs learning, and then the misunderstood words become piled higher and deeper.

Organization

Students must be taught how to be good students and to take pride in their work. Most of the students that I have taught in the Learning Resource classes have organization problems. Organization is a prime ingredient in personal success. Without it, one is lost and cannot attain his goals in life. Therefore, this is a skill that has to be taught. Students must learn the purpose for organization. It is fairly easy to recognize the disorganized student, because he is the Santa who comes loaded down with a worn-out backpack overflowing with all his books and papers from the entire year, sometimes last year as well. He generally has no pencils, though a stub of one may turn up once he empties everything all over the table and floor. He has months old assignments, wrinkled, dirty, and torn, sometimes completed or half done but never turned in for credit. He is the student who takes twenty minutes to get ready for class and by then has missed half of the instructions for the day's assignment. The remedy is to put him on a gradient. It is going to require a shakedown periodically of his backpack. Have him look at all the junk that was stuffed and sometimes lost for weeks in the dark recesses of his pack. It is interesting what one discovers as everything is unloaded on a table. Then organize with him the binders and papers. Suggest to him and his parents that he purchase different colored folders for each subject and put them in a single binder. Train him to use an agenda planner with his homework assignments. Try to involve the parents in supervising his organization before he leaves for school every morning and again when he returns home. Then have the student check in with you on a regular schedule and finally on an intermittent schedule.

One year when I was teaching at a middle school, I had a student come to me before school for a shakedown, after lunch, and at the end of the day. Finally, he got where he could get himself organized after this routine drill went on for about a year. So there is hope!

Definitions

We have a category for communication impaired in special education, but all my students and a few of my colleagues are communication disordered to some degree, and it's always based on the misunderstood word. Everything is so complicated and high sounding about what the student's problem could be that it is no wonder the teachers do not know how to proceed; neither, of course, do the psychologists or psychiatrists. The psychiatrists state that the problem for example is PDD. What does that mean? Pervasive Developmental Disorder? How do you fix it? Define the word and you get—pervade—to be present or have the tendency to be present throughout, and developmental—to become affected with, grow or expand, and disorder—an ailment that affects the mind or body. Little wonder it cannot be treated; those creating this definition do not know what it is either. The DSM manual gets thicker and thicker,

Learning Disabilities: The Myth

and more students are diagnosed with more and more disabilities, and the frustration mounts because it cannot be fixed; at least not like this.

Teachers have their own misunderstood notions on these students and what to do with them. Many believe that the textbook must be covered and so they fly up the gradient scale, making it steeper and steeper until all those at the bottom are lost in chaos and swirling misunderstanding. The teacher then says the student does not pay attention; he is just goofing off or not motivated. Then these students will commit acts against the environment to justify what they consider crimes against them.

Application

Why are we graduating illiterates? There is way too much significance and not enough application, that is why. Western education gets totally bogged down in significances, and very well leaves out the application. Anything we learn, we ought to be able to apply and demonstrate that knowledge. If we cannot, then we have not learned it.

Students do need some theory and reasons for studying a subject, but then the rest should be devoted to application. This is why students are becoming more turned off to education. They do not see the relevancy to their lives and the usefulness of what has been dished out in generous portions over their twelve years of schooling. We call students lazy, unmotivated. Well, yes, they are. They must be taught to be students. That is not just a role that they come into naturally by osmosis. It is tough work to study; it is their job, just as it is ours to be a teacher.

Do we have a workable definition for education? Maybe this is part and parcel of the problem. How do we educate when we do not having a working definition.

Do we clear up our own misunderstood words? Ben, one of the students in my second-year reading class, was able to determine that his U.S. history teacher had a misunderstood word by the symptoms he displayed. The teacher looked up at the class after stumbling over the word to see if anyone was looking and quickly looked down again. Are we embarrassed to look up a word with our students? Do we require them to clear their words? Behind every comprehension deficit, math error, and failure is a misunderstood word. Have students to find and define their misunderstood words and learn them to full conceptual understanding.

Understanding

All people want to know, so it is a natural for students to want to know. To know something is an act of survival and it is something that no one can take from us. I was told this as a child, believed it, and never forgot it. I have been seeking to know things and understand them all my life. Knowing is free for the taking in most Western and democratic societies. Knowing does not stand alone, though, and goes hand in glove with application.

Any student has a natural curiosity about life, but somewhere along the way, he was suppressed through suggestion, act, or deed, or perhaps told he could not have or reach his goal. This began to block his knowingness and willingness to know. It became a painful experience for him through invalidation and impaired communication. He ceased to look at things with curiosity

All students can learn on a gradient; just find the gradient and proceed. It's going to take some longer than others obviously, but we need to identify carefully what it is that we want all students to know, and that might not be all the chapters and theories in a history or science book, for instance. It might be what can be applied. This is what many rebel against. It is okay for students to know important reasons and theory, but it is not okay for students to spend hours and hours learning useless information that can never be applied. Leave that for the philosophers. Students need to know something and be able to demonstrate understanding through application; otherwise, what good is all this schooling?

Recently, a colleague sent out an e-mail message calling for help in locating a good doctor. She explained that in Italy not too long ago, an American cardiologist had examined her and told her she had a very serious heart condition that required her to be evacuated immediately to the United States for specialized care. Upon arrival at her destination and further examination, she was found to be in perfect health without a sign of heart trouble. After backtracking

Learning Disabilities: The Myth

and investigating, it was discovered that the doctor in Italy had not hooked up the heart machine. A frightening thought if this were the cardiologist on duty in surgery! Imagine what a wonderful world to live in if everyone understood the key words on his job.

Memory Work

Students do not memorize facts and information any more. Well, some things must be memorized, there is no other way. For example, you want your airline pilot to have memorized his routine thoroughly before he takes that 747 off the ground, and then you want him to understand the theory or the concept of flight dynamics, terrorism, and emergency procedures. There is no room for error. You want precision. Then you want it where he can analyze any problem and take the right action immediately. The same goes for your surgeon, the engineer, and your teacher.

The *experts* from the universities would have us believe that students cannot get better and, therefore, they must learn survival skills. They say that if they did not *get* it (decoding, grammar, computation) early, they are not likely to get it later. Confidential files are filled with discrepancies: one examiner writes that a student has information processing deficits, only to be refuted by the next examiner, and nearly always disproved in the classroom. To survive, these LI students need to read and memorize certain facts and data. Repetition and drill on important facts and theories are necessary with the end result of application.

At the same time, students must be addressed as unique beings and spirits, not as people who evolved from mud. They are trying to survive in the academic world and once they are given hope and are taught how to study, they can survive in life. That is not to say that it is easy, because it is not. These students very often are quite reactive, and that needs fixing. It can be fixed when they experience a little success, firmness, fairness, and a plan for learning. You will see that they fall right into line when the boundaries are set, they have been given work that has a purpose, and they are told about that purpose, and are taught the barriers to study.

Make sure that you, the teacher, have a purpose, are organized, and follow a plan. Students do not do well during study if there is slack time. Keep the momentum going, being sure that they clear all misunderstood words. Be a resource and be resourceful. The student will do his own learning and quickly throw away the crutch that has been provided in the field of special education. Know that he can do it, and see to it.

Application

Nearly every year, I have worked with students with disabilities who excelled in sports like football and other activities such as cheerleading and drama. They were leaders in extra curricular activities; I mean the top in the school. Why? I believe that it is not because it does not require reading, and not because they have the need to excel in something. It is because of the application involved in these activities. Some professionals would have us believe that it is some sort of self-esteem issue. They say it is because these students cannot excel in the classroom, and therefore, look elsewhere.

For sure these students benefit from these activities, but the activities are no substitute for what they should be learning and understanding in the classroom. I have no doubt that probably every one of these students had some degree of reading deficit, with loads of misunderstood words. All of these students could learn, and learn well, if the study gradient is right, study technology is in, and they can learn to apply what they know. Students build self-esteem by understanding and applying what they have learned. They feel competent as beings.

It is natural to want to apply what one learns. The problem in the classroom is all the data that teachers think are important, like the entire book. We have all known the teacher who feels compelled to cover the book and at a mad rate. We also know the one who assigns a chapter to read in world history, followed by the test from the publisher's test bank, after assigning all the vocabulary, all the questions, and all the exercises at the end of each unit. Rarely in discussion in the class is a student allowed to evaluate a datum to see if it is real for him. If the book said so, it must be so. I remember when my son was in the third grade and watched a film on the solar system. When the film was over, he disputed something that was in the film, and the teacher chastised him. Though humiliated, he held his ground and pointed out the film was made in the 1960s, and this was already twenty-five years or so later. You see, he read voraciously about the solar system, and this data did not fit with what he knew to be so.

Why do we sink the student in a sea of data through constant input straight out of the book augmented by handouts? All of the information in any textbook is not worth knowing or remembering. Sort through it and decide what it is you want the student to learn and focus on that. Have him learn it cold. Allow the student to evaluate the important pieces of information that we want him to know. Have him examine it, restate it, and come up with different and novel ways to use it. Then he owns it; otherwise, he will ultimately resist this data, or become a glib student in order to get a good grade, or run off, or drop out of school altogether.

We have to understand and apply what we know. Here is an example of what I mean by the glib student. One of the algebra teachers that I work with was puzzled when one of her best students got confused on her "Big Dig" project. The project was on the metric system, and students were to measure each person's tibia, humerus, or radius, and graph the results based on the estimate of the height of a person. The report was very well written, and the graphs were colorful and neat and labeled appropriately. By taking a closer look at the graphs, my colleague realized this student's figures and graphs did not make any sense. "I just do not see how she could have messed up here," she said. "You can look at the graphs and see that they do not make any sense." It was obvious to me that this student had not understood metrics. She had misunderstood a word or concept and, as a result, could not apply!

In the fall of this school year, I interviewed Joe, a new student to the high school, and his mother to determine what I could do to help him. He was about to turn twenty-one in January and was trying to get enough credits to reenter the New York City school system to graduate. He said he had dropped out for two years, had worked flipping hamburgers at McDonald's, and now had decided he needed a better life. "I'm about to become a daddy," he said, "and I need to graduate and make something of my life." When questioned further, he said that he would like to take the ASVAB (Armed Services Vocational Abilities Battery), an entry test for the United States military services, and enter the Air Force. He admitted he had had a reading problem all his life. "My eleven-year-old brother reads better than I do," he said. He said that most of his

Learning Disabilities: The Myth

classes had not made much sense, and that it was hard to sit and listen to so much talk. He added that he was good at using his hands and wanted to do things, not sit through boring lectures that he could not understand. His Performance Intelligence Quotient (PIQ) on the Wechsler Intelligence Scale—Revised bore this out with an IQ of 130, way above the average.

Then there is the story of Robert, the intellectually borderline case, who was clearly burned out by all the significances in the school curriculum. I was teaching in a middle school in the early days of my career, in a neighborhood with a low socio-economic clientele and school attendance was a big problem among others. Robert had been absent for several days and when he finally did show up, I asked, "Robert, where've you been?"

"Been with my PO [probation officer]," Robert replied.

"What have you been doing?" I asked.

"Been robbin'," said Robert.

"Robbing what?"

"Filin' station [gas station]."

"For what?"

"Bottle caps."

"Why?"

"So's I kin' sell 'um."

Obviously, I'd not stressed the value of cold, hard cash! Robert was an eight-hour-a-day retarded we used to call it, or Educationally Retarded. He was trying to apply, because what he was getting at school was not helping him be a better, more prepared citizen. Sadly, these students turn to crime, getting into trouble with the law all too often when they have not learned something that can be applied or that can help them solve the problems of life. Prisons are filled with former, burned-out students who could not read and had misunderstood key words in their school work and misunderstood words about their roles as beings.

On Understanding

The biggest stumbling block to success in anything is not being able to understand and apply knowledge. It is the misunderstood word that confuses and confounds teachers and students in school and in life. Clearing up these misunderstood words and concepts can help us reach new vistas of understanding and scale new heights of learning. One of the first things I tell my students is that they must learn to find their misunderstood words in a subject and clear them up before they can progress. I tell the students that in order to clear up ignorance and stupidity on something, they have to find out what it is that they do not understand. I begin with a demonstration, and have the students look up the word student in the dictionary. Clearing words is going to take a lot of repetition and drill to make it part of the routine, especially if the students are not accustomed to defining words.

Nevertheless, just introducing the idea of misunderstood words and talking about it is an important first step. Have plenty of good dictionaries on hand and start on day one by discussing and appreciating the English language. Make certain that they have a good idea about the function of a dictionary and how it is used. Many do not understand guidewords and how to quickly follow the sequence of the alphabet to find the correct word. Talk about all the various definitions, the importance of word derivations, word usage, synonyms, and idioms. Make that dictionary a tool by making it understood by the students, and have them use it.

Find out what has been misunderstood in whatever subject the student has deficiencies. Training the student to never go past a word that he does not know is of vital importance, then locating the troublesome area of study: the time when he had his very first non-comprehension. Just before this, you will find the basic misunderstood word. Get it cleared up and then move forward. This is difficult in a resource room where the subjects and assignments are heavy and suppressive, but if you can teach a student this skill, you have gone forward in removing the crutch of learned helplessness.

In the beginning of the year we talk about the roles of the student and teacher; then students look up the definitions of both. Next, we define education and study. Education is defined as the knowledge or skill obtained or developed by a learning process. *(Second College Edition: The American Heritage Dictionary, c. 1991)*. Education is not defined adequately because application is left out. Perhaps, that is why some teachers have misunderstood the word education; they never learned that application was the end result of it.

Find out what a student has misunderstood in a lesson or subject and clear it up right away. Have them find the definition of the misunderstood word and proceed to clear the word. Next, have them read all the definitions, make sentences with the word, then find the definition that is appropriate for the context. They can work in pairs to accomplish this but should make ten or more sentences each. Then have them read the word derivation and the word usages such as synonyms and so forth. You may have to repeat this from time to time because it will take a number of times over this procedure to get it down. Be sure to follow the precise procedures in Hubbard's *Basic Study Manual* for excellent results.

Once you have trained word clearing over a semester, always requiring students to clear their misunderstood words, you will see a miraculous increase in using the dictionary. Always have a student pass out dictionaries before the bell rings so that time is not wasted later on. They will begin breaking the word down and finding the base word to study; this is a great asset in reading. The concept of finding the misunderstood word is carried over to other classes and the content areas. For example, one day Walter, one of my seniors, asked me to help him with a problem in his Advanced Algebra class. Here I am on shaky ground because I do not do Advanced Algebra every day nor am I a math teacher; however, my students expect me to help them with everything, and so I do. I said, "Walter, let's find your misunderstood word. Go back to where you began having the problem." He showed me and then we backtracked some more because the misunderstanding occurred before he became confused. It is always somewhere right about where he was understanding, and then he came across a misunderstood word and went blank. He reviewed an example that he had skipped over and found the word that was giving him some trouble. We read together the previous page and reviewed the examples. Then he proceeded to understand

and came forward to the problem he was working on. "Oh, I get it now," he said. "Thanks!" Works every time.

I talk about the physiological and mental symptoms of the misunderstood word (although there are about twenty-six, I only mention the main ones) and what they can do to someone. I also teach my students about the ten different ways a word can be misunderstood. One student last year from one of my classes became so good with identifying her own misunderstood words that she could identify her teacher's misunderstood words. One day she came in with a story about her English teacher. She said that her teacher was reading an article to the class and halfway through, she kind of stumbled on a word and looked around to see if anyone had caught it. Jen said, "She had a blank look on her face, then quickly looked down. I know she had a misunderstood word and was embarrassed about it. She should have asked the class to clear it with her!" So students do know when we do not know!

Teaching them to find their own misunderstood word is not easy at first. Many have become so dependent on the teacher and are not self-determined at all about their own learning. This dependency is a problem that the education system creates. We spend so much time lecturing and having students take in information that students become hypnotized. Data goes in and then comes out on demand during exams. One student in particular comes to mind when I think of dependence on the teacher. She hated math and felt she absolutely could not do it. She was a product of a crazy mother who punished her regularly for being in special education and a father who had no active involvement with his daughter's learning. He and the mother had been divorced for some time, and the daughter lived with the mother. Christa could not do a single problem in Introduction to Algebra independently. In fact, she could not even get her name on the paper in the correct place. Besides being shy and without confidence, she actually stank from poor hygiene, so sitting side by side with her took a fair amount of courage and perseverance on my part. For an entire year, I had her sit beside me as we went over the algebra one painful step at a time in order to find her misunderstood. I would do the problem for her, and she would observe and then copy it. After some practice, she would write the beginning of the

Learning Disabilities: The Myth

problem and try a step she thought might be correct. This would continue for the first quarter, the second quarter, the third quarter, until finally, she got it. She was beginning to find her misunderstood words and take on more responsibility for learning algebra now that she had a plan, a way to proceed. Her learning rate was enormously slow, but she learned. By the end of the year, I only had to sit in the vicinity of Christa and check her work for occasional mistakes, which decreased. She was able to confront the problems, find her mistakes, and solve them. This was a great strategy that worked quite well with this student, although she needed more opportunities to apply the learned data. By her tenth-grade year, she could go to the Algebra I teacher, get some answers to her questions, and proceed independently. Now in her third year, she works completely independent of me and will probably move out of the program by midyear. The gradient approach, clearing misunderstood words, and supplying mass when necessary worked. It's marvelous! The only problem really that Christa is going to encounter is that the math curriculum is so heavy with worksheets and text coverage and low on application, though the school is about to add algebra labs. Nevertheless, she will have gotten her credit, which is a win for her.

Most students these days want to go to college because that is what society is telling them. Never mind that they struggled all the way through high school or never bothered to do homework or made the slightest effort to improve. (I am not talking about those who do.) One cannot jump from A to Z when reciting the alphabet unless one has repeated all the letters in between. The same goes for study. It is like a ladder that I illustrate on the board when I hold parent conferences. The student has to take one step after the next; if he tries to skip one, he gets shaky and is likely to fall off. An example: Tim wanted to go to college but had severe reading and written language deficits as well as great difficulties in math. His SAT (Scholastic Aptitude Test) scores for college admission were dismal, less than two hundred combined for both verbal and math out of a possible 1600. He was missing a whole lot of steps in between. I recommended a more realistic approach: take the predictor ASVAB (Armed Services Vocational Abilities Battery) test for the military services that identifies interests and skills and matches the two. The minimum score is thirty-one for the army and navy and forty for the air force. This was a more realistic approach when he made a score of twenty-six. Now he could study up on math and take the predictor test again in a few weeks. If he had the minimum score, then he would immediately take the ASVAB.

For two years Sasha worked on a gradient, looking up her misunderstood words and using mass as she needed it in her reading and written language, until she was able to fly on her own. As it turned out, she became one of the top students in the regular English 12 class. I was not surprised the day she charged into the room with her senior thesis, grinning from ear to ear, and presented her paper to me. "Look!" she exclaimed and pushed her research paper on dolphins across my desk. "He even liked my argument." She earned a ninety-eight! "Clearing up my misunderstood words made a big difference," she said. Now words from English literature are ordinary to her. Not bad for a student who was considered "language impaired"!

Students become discipline problems and often leave school not only because of misunderstood words and concepts, but also from broken communication cycles. At the beginning of the year, my ninth-graders generally have a settling-in time and need a lot of good control and training with communication drills to get them on track and focused. It is important that the teacher know how to acknowledge students properly and get good communication going among and between students. Communication must be taught; it is not a given. As communication improves so does one's communication with objects, environments, and with the universe. It brings one into the present moment. It makes a difference in school. A student can understand his purpose for a subject, can communicate with that subject *and* the teacher. Good communication brings understanding.

What the Teacher Confronts

Teacher Stress

Teachers have to confront a lot when they enter education these days. We confront societal ills and are expected to fix everything. These social problems along with the permissiveness in most public schools and the lack of a proper technology to teach students *how* to learn, lead to an invalidation of the discipline of teaching itself. Teachers are expected to encourage proper dress, teach manners and responsibility, help eradicate drug problems, control and prevent sexually transmitted diseases, change negative behaviors, and so forth. At the same time, teachers are expected to teach to the standards set forth in the curriculum, address the needs of all the students, and ensure that students make high scores on school-wide and national achievement tests.

The truth is that we are taking on all the responsibilities of society for the rearing of its children, yet we are not doing a commendable job. We cannot teach because we are not allowed to be self-determined in our profession anymore. Someone from above dictates how it is, leaving very little time for us to do what we do best: teach students. The student cannot learn because he does not have the proper technology.

The field of special education is believed to be the field of highest burnout in the entire teaching profession. Why? No matter the effort, there is limited student progress. This is due to the suppressive system which loads the teacher down and does not value teaching. The parents do not consistently support the programs, students lack motivation, regular-class teachers want these students out of their classes, and support staff rarely have workable plans. Many of the special education teachers change teaching jobs after only a year or so; some even prefer unemployment to the high stress. Nowadays, multicultural students and many with limited English proficiency are thrown into special education classrooms when all else fails. Once identified as special education students, all are placed back into the regular classroom, where the failure syndrome continues. The only difference is the *label* has changed. No matter the modifications made, the gradient of the curriculum is too steep and the misunderstood words and concepts snowball. Some do get better grades, graduate, and even go on for further training, but they carry with them a void, a black hole in their learning.

Why such a mess? Policymakers, influenced by those at the university level who do their research in their ivory towers of learning, barely spend minutes in the school systems they write about so expertly. Oh, the professors have marvelous theories, albeit non-workable. They fix education with their documented research and get funding for grants and more unworkable plans but rarely darken the doors of a public school. If they had spent more time in the field rather than leaving this up to their graduate students, they might have realized that their research did not translate into anything beneficial at the school level.

Some teachers do give up on teaching altogether but stay on because they cannot confront another job. They stay and say, well, it is this or that and that things are never going to get any better. They do not realize the source of their stress is the invalidation that comes from a system that needs over-hauling in the worst way. They deal with the new plan from the education hierarchy for student achievement every two years or so, having never been asked how to fix it. This new deal came from someone or some company trying to make a whole lot of dough off their program, or some politician with his advisory panel looking for free publicity, or some experts from the prestigious universities wanting to publish their new theories. None, I mean none, ever asked the workers in the field; it would be heresy to do so. During my twenty-five years of teaching, I was never asked how a particular decision would impact my teaching or program, nor was I asked what I thought needed to be changed to make it better. Decisions about curriculum, teaching methods and education in general always came from some other wiser source, usually, some politician in education who came around on a fact-finding mission. On occasion, a traveling fact finder will say he wants input, but ignores it when it is offered. He does not want a workable plan, he wants votes!

The Student

The student comes to school and to special education with a myriad of problems and diagnoses. Given all this, it is next to impossible to sort it all out when one sees the chaos and confusion swirling around and throughout the student's education history. Best to start from scratch and ignore the fiction, because that is what about 90 percent of it is. I ignore the canned IEPs from the various computer programs; it does not help me teach the student. What is going to work is having a look at the student, so I just observe and start from there. Where is the student academically and emotionally? Make your own evaluation of how the student really is and based on your experience and observations. Listen carefully to what he is saying; he'll provide you with a wealth of information if you look and listen. How does he communicate: Does he look you in the eye? Is he communicating with a body part or avoiding looking at you completely? Has he duplicated what you said? Is he in present time? Check the reading level, determine the deficient sub-skills in reading, and you have a pretty good picture of where he is.

Place them on the gradient scale of learning, put your intention into it that the student will learn and begin. Explain and teach the student to clear all words, use the clay table and demo kits, and insist he learn important data 100 percent. Students want solutions that work; they want to apply the knowledge they gain. They want to escape a life of illiteracy, drugs, and whatever else is darkening their days and preventing their success and happiness in life. Recognize this and you are on the right track to seeking a solution and salvaging a human being.

We are graduating illiterates because of the misunderstood words in education and the burdensome significance from the top down in general. Millions of dollars are spent every year to hire more psychologists, buy more materials, and pay more assessors to identify and fix the problems. But the problems do not get fixed; we bog down deeper and deeper. Nearly every year we change something about how it is: new forms, more paperwork, different computer programs, more software, and revised procedures. And the next year, more assessment teams. The rationale, presumably, is that there are far too many students who have disabilities that are in need of identification. But there is no plan when they arrive unless the individual teacher makes the plan. In my entire teaching career I have never ever been offered any training specifically in my field to be a better teacher, until this year when I had a workshop on computer software for SE students. What I had to know, I had to find out on my own, and thus began my quest for methods to teach these students.

Most students come to school with a curiosity and a desire to learn. If we can check their behavior and get them moving on the correct gradient, they will learn, and there would be no need to constantly sort the students by disability, because there is no such thing as a learning disability for the vast majority of students. So I am talking about the vast majority of students labeled and placed in classes where they learn less and lose hope. Can they lose hope in regular classes? Of course they can, if the material is way over their heads and they are allowed to gloss over misunderstood words. Any student can learn, provided good control has been established and the three barriers to study are addressed. Even those with genetic defects and traumatic injuries can learn, but usually on a very low gradient. Only the rate of learning separates students in their ability to acquire and use knowledge.

Good control means establishing the boundaries very firmly. This provides a large measure of security for the students and helps the student become more self-determined. Teach students to recognize that life extends from self to family to group to mankind to environment (plants and animals) to the physical universe and to self as a spirit. Students must be taught that responsibility and ethical behavior affect our survival and that of life itself. Teach students to make decisions based on the greatest good for each one of these areas. When we leave out any of these, we fail in life.

Last year, my students were involved in so much unethical activity that I was about to walk out—I mean just leave. Moral confusion was great: hatred, promiscuity, drugs, violence, theft, and lack of respect for property. They were stealing from me, each other, from visiting sports teams; one was dealing in drugs; another bludgeoned two other students, using a steel lock on one that could have killed him and kicking the other in the face, before being apprehended.

Learning Disabilities: The Myth

Another student set up an orgy for sex in the boy's bathroom, by invitation only. Some of my girls were lying about each other and getting in catfights, lying to me, and stealing from the local store. Homework and doing class work were minor issues when we look at these ethical considerations. I was thinking, *It's not my job*, but it was; otherwise, who would do it. I had to accept responsibility for their ethics training but do it in such a way as not to encroach on their private religious beliefs. I recalled that as a schoolgirl, some notion of morality was instilled in us in school with prayer and verses from the Bible. During my tenure as a teacher, there has been no touching on moral values, and certainly no time is spent teaching them to our children. The home is supposed to do it, right? Wrong! Some do; most do not. They leave it up to the school or figure that their children will learn it by osmosis.

William Kilpatrick, author of *Why Johnny Can't Tell Right from Wrong*, states that psychology based–values education teaches our children "a totally non-judgmental attitude," and "no time is spent providing moral guidance or forming character. No reason is given why a boy or girl should want to be good in the first place." The result then, according to Kilpatrick, is that young people "come away with the impression that even the most basic values are matters of dispute." My classroom had become a living hell, and I realized that the question about moral values had not been resolved for these young people, and I could not go on. I adopted *The Way to Happiness,* a booklet written by writer and humanitarian L. Ron Hubbard that outlines a practical approach to happiness by discussing twenty-one moral precepts. These precepts form a secular code that would be applicable in any culture or by people from any religion or none. Each precept is followed by its description and how it can be applied in everyday life. It is based on common sense and can readily be understood and used. It outlines the universal principles of brotherhood and love and borrows from thousands of years of all the great religious teachings.

What I do: A precept is posted and discussed and reviewed until the students have full understanding and can conceptualize what each precept is. We discuss each one and define any unknown words. The students give examples of each precept once it is understood and talk about their responsibility on each one. These precepts are spread out over the course of a year, with a new one being introduced once a week. I can see that students are becoming kinder to one another in my classroom, and the unethical behavior has disappeared. I do not know if it is a result of reading the precepts or not, but it is my intention that I am doing something to help.

I tried everything that I could get my hands on to educate these students that appeared uneducable given the longevity of the problems and their down-tone emotional level and self-devaluation. The behavior problems always surfaced in one form or another. For some of the students, it was practicing wrong lessons learned well, for some, it was learned helplessness, and for others, it was lack of motivation created by apathy toward learning. Their parents push for special education because they tend to be burned out by the time the student reaches high school and are more than willing for someone else to shoulder the responsibility of making the student do his homework.

I never knew that I made a difference in any student's life until I began teaching them how to confront life's problems and work out things for themselves. The gains from one student alone last year were astounding. The gradient approach works not only in academics but every aspect of our life; it is a vital tool for communication. Sasha was having difficulty with her parents getting them to understand that she wanted to take charge of her life. What to do? Instead of the big fights that they had been having recently, she proceeded very slowly getting them used to the idea that decisions about her future career, for example, were decisions that she needed to make, right or wrong.

Government Spending

The U.S. government under President Bush has reached its highest level of spending on special education, $8.5 billion. Still we are graduating illiterates or near-illiterates, students who have been pressed into special education (Associated Press, Washington, D.C., March 19, 2003). About 6.3 million children receive special help currently in the United States. The IDEA, the Individuals with Disabilities Education Act of 1975, the law that promised appropriate education for all is being reauthorized. It is to be aligned with the No Child Left Behind Act. The law is intended to reduce the number of students who are misidentified as disabled by speeding intervention for low-achieving students and by allowing school districts to spend federal money on preventive instructional programs aimed at averting the future need for comprehensive special education services. The Bush administration criticized the special education law for emphasizing adherence to its many technical provisions, rather than overall student achievement. Amen. Democrats, of course, oppose the measure and say that the proposal of the House Republicans shortchanges parents and due process rights. All these laws are passed, actions are taken, and education is still spiraling downward. The paperwork mounts and lawsuits fly. And still Johnny can't read or write.

Throw out one program that cost millions of dollars and adopt another that costs even more. Millions of dollars are spent annually for teacher training, new programs, and textbooks. Why then do the test statistics decline in the United States? Mathematics and science, especially, are taking a nosedive. There is something that we can do about this problem and the cost is minimal. We can spend money on some good dictionaries and train teachers in Study Technology and communication. That is it!

Just last year, I was forced to accept $3,000 of taxpayer money spent on junk that I did not want nor could not use. I refused the money when I was not allowed to purchase scientific calculators for my students. Although my administrator supported me initially, she acquiesced when those more knowledgeable leaders from the district put pressure on the school to accept these worthless materials. A total waste! A box of phonics books is an example of some of the materials designated for my program, along with other canned programs. All are stored in a closet to be tossed at some later date by the next teacher. Now this year during budget cutbacks, I could only get $100 to support my program!

Committees

We solve our problems by committee meetings, where we get all our reactive minds together to come up with a solution to what we consider to be the problems in our schools. More often than not, the good thinker with the creative mind and good ideas is squashed. He is squashed because he usually does not fit the conservative mainstream. The mainstream thinking is aligned with the middle class and 'what is best for all' without examining what is best for all. What is best for all is often decided by politicians, special interest groups, and universities far removed from our school. Because it is democratic?

For instance, we have a school improvement plan, as do most schools, I am sure. This committee creates all kinds of initiatives and programs to teach students to ask certain types of high-level thinking questions. What is really a wonder is that there is no plan to see that the student is self-determined on this data and that he has cleared his misunderstood words. No, he will not be *able* to analyze data until these two issues are handled. Most importantly, we have adopted no plan to teach a student how to learn. Our assumption is that they come to school already knowing how to study.

A colleague told me this week, "All I have time to do these days is check off a list, all minutiae, and nothing related to lesson plans, working with students, or conferring with colleagues about students." She was feeling exhausted and invalidated as are most faculty members I have interviewed. Teachers become apathetic after a few years of attending meetings that come to no end and implementing wrong decisions made by others. Oh, I am sure that there are some out there that would say this is blasphemous and that their school has handled all sorts of things with committees. This may be true, but then they should share this with the rest of us.

What generally happens is that a suppressive person takes over, someone operating at the covert hostile range, and says with a big smile, "This is for the good of all," knowing full well that it is never going to solve anything. Reactive thinking of most everyone is stirred up, and analytical thinking goes out the window. The awful plan is accepted and the true thinkers become apathetic about the whole thing. A few creative and bright thinkers should be managing a committee and directing it. You ask, "Where is the democracy here?" A good example would be to ask, "What color should we paint the wall?" Go around the room and ask each person. Their responses mostly differ. Fair might be to paint the wall plaid. The majority response was green, but that is really an awful color and makes a lot of people sick. Get the idea?

Solutions

Teachers want solutions to the existing problems in education! They cannot find solutions because they do not have a spare minute to think about them. Most decisions regulating teaching are made somewhere else and are handed down by committees for other committees to implement. And these committees probably got it from higher ups who maybe got it from the universities, whose education faculties are busy writing "somebody said that somebody else said" or politicians, even less informed, are creating their *own* fiction about what ails our schools. These decisions, many suppressive and burdensome, impact how the teachers at the local schools attempt to handle problems. They no longer have confidence in their ability to observe and come up with something that works. They have to make sure that it has the approval of this one or that one, that it is in line with all the various regulations and curriculum standards, state or system standards, district and local interpretations and so forth. No wonder teachers are exhausted these days. Like my colleague said, they *are* busy checking off lists!

Here is an example of the *perceived* problem at our local high school and solutions: Nearly 40 to 60 percent of our student body is consistently making Ds and Fs, and our faculty intends to solve this problem. By union vote, the faculty *will* solve the problem by changing the schedule from one of duration to one of frequency. "We need contact with students every day," they cried. I had heard this cry before. At my last school the faculty sought to improve student performance by changing from a schedule of frequency to one of duration. "We need increased contact time for each class so we can *cover* all the material." Neither worked because the problem had not been identified. The grades are a *result* of the problem and the problem is related to the barriers of study. In Washington, D. C., officials of my school system tried to solve the problem of why so many students were failing Introductory Algebra system wide with a curriculum change. They dropped the Introductory Algebra classes altogether and offered Algebra I as the beginning math course in high school. Then to support students who required it, a computerized Algebra Lab program was added. Even so, it has not helped the students with deficiencies in math that I teach. Another strategy that was implemented midway last year for those deficient in Algebra I the first semester was a repeat in a speeded up version second semester of Algebra I, before continuing the regular second semester.

The gradient in Algebra I is way too steep due to basic misunderstood words and concepts. The *patch-up* approach gets them by, but do they retain and can they apply at the next level? Many of these basic Algebra concepts were covered in Introductory Algebra. Even in Introductory Algebra, some of my students needed a lower gradient! Now with the curriculum change and steep gradient, their chances of success in the high school math curriculum are dim; some had to be removed from Algebra I altogether this year. Recently, one of the math teachers had a solution for this new dilemma. Those who make an F must repeat Algebra I. Did I mention some were failing Algebra Lab also, and others were making passing grades in Algebra Lab but failing Algebra I? This year a high percentage are making D's and F's in Geometry because they never got their misunderstood words, symbols and concepts cleared up in Algebra and now the pace is snowballing with all the geometry words. Of course, spatial understanding is a problem when the students have not had sufficient mass to provide understanding.

Everyone is looking for a solution and coming up with the wrong one because the problem has yet to be identified. Presumably to motivate students on the first day of school to reach greater heights of academic awareness, an administrative decision was made to blare an unbelievably loud song, "We Will Rock You" by Queen over the intercom. Later on, I asked a few students what they thought about this. One stated, "It sounded like music in the grocery store when I go shopping (in the American store)." Another said, "It was stupid!" Another replied, "I did not pay any attention to it." Then I asked, "Did it help you learn better?" They replied with a resounding response, "No!"

By the end of the first quarter this year, our school still has about the same number of D's and F's that we have always had. Realizing

Learning Disabilities: The Myth

the continuing downward spiral of grades, during second quarter the principal has proposed a new remedy to fix the skipped gradient from Introductory Science to Biology. The new solution will be after school tutoring sessions in biology. See, we skipped a gradient and are trying frantically to patch things up, especially for the freshmen. Oh, their grades may improve, and it will no doubt help some get by, but is it going to help them be able to apply this knowledge? And what about the next level in science? Do we start all over again because the problem has not been identified? Maybe someone else can figure out this wisdom; I cannot.

Individualization as a Solution

My system has spent millions of taxpayers' dollars on training. Most of us have had opportunities for both good and marginal training in many different exotic places. A few of the good workshops and courses that I attended were Writer's Workshop, AIMS (integrating science with math) and the New Math Standards. These three were enormously useful, and students benefited as a result, because application was the intent. As teachers, we enjoyed all these wonderful vacations with extra pay that accompanied these summer appointments. Only now, these good initiatives along with others have been discarded and replaced by something else. They are replaced because students still are not making the gains expected on national and system wide tests, no matter the intervention. The missing ingredient is obvious, but remains hidden to those who refuse to look.

Most students come to school with a curiosity about learning, but few know how to go about it. The student must be taught *how* to learn! First, we must recognize that students learn at different rates. Then, in order to teach a student how to learn, we must know what can block the student from progressing. We must recognize the mental and physiological symptoms that accompany too steep of a study gradient, lack of mass and the misunderstood word and know the remedies precisely. Students must be taught these symptoms and three barriers to study along with the remedies. Once learned, the student is placed on the correct gradient and proceeds at his own rate. The problem, naturally, is that teachers cannot control the gradient of the curriculum.

Study Technology is a system of individualized study that is the answer to our current dilemma in education. Its success has been demonstrated in my classroom and in classrooms around the globe. It is a system of study that could bring enormous savings in dollars. More importantly, this technology could save us as a nation.

The Student as a Spiritual Being

Carolina handed me her biology project and promptly said, "They have a big misunderstood on this." I looked up, eager to find out who had a misunderstood on what and said, "Who has a misunderstood about what?" She pointed to the papers before me that included a graph she had been working on and some lengthy articles from an Internet site assigned by her biology teacher. The project was to graph the ascent of man from the beginning to *Homo sapiens*, listing the time and characteristics. She said, "I did not come from all that." I said, "I know." She smiled and we proceeded to arrange the graph in order of who came first and began to plow through all the data based on "The Theory of Natural Selection."

Students are spiritual beings and instinctively know this. They know that they are something more than what is implied directly or indirectly in the theories put forth in biology. If they are allowed to recognize this and encouraged to know that they have infinite capacity with infinite ability, they will flourish with the proper guidance. They will know that the spirit can overpower this mind and body. They will realize that they live infinitely.

It is next to impossible to teach a student well without recognizing their spirit and beingness. Fortunately, I recognized this early on when teaching students with different capabilities, personalities, and motivation. If I addressed their spirit, they would respond. They did respond and related to me in a way that I had not been able to explain or understand until now.

Sasha kept getting better and better, until one day toward the end of her senior year she remarked, "I can do anything I put my mind to." Giving her the tools of learning were one thing; giving her tools that she could apply in life were quite another.

Jamie Jon

Jamie Jon wrote awkwardly in very large block letters that were nearly illegible. He wrote reams of pages; his mother said that he had drawers filled with his writings. But no one could read what he wrote. And no one took the time to have *him* read it. Jamie Jon was labeled autistic, which meant a whole lot of different things to a whole lot of different specialists. His records were filled with descriptions of his multiple disabilities, some in agreement and some not, none of which gave one a single clue as to how to teach him. Physically, he was not very attractive. His face was covered with acne, he had a cleft palate, wore braces, had hair that would not lay straight when parted, slid his feet along the floor when he walked, and rubbed various parts of his private anatomy in public. Although his affect was flat and he laughed inappropriately, he was pleasant and had no outbursts or overt behaviors that would interfere with the learning of others. Yet nothing in his individual education plan seemed to fit him.

When Jamie Jon, at age fourteen, enrolled as a new eighth-grade student in my program, I had students from eighth to twelfth grades with mild problems; I realized he was not going to fit. Besides, other students did not like the idea of having such a student amongst them. It labeled them as retarded by association, and he looked and acted so different. Acceptance by the others was not going to be easy, and I just dreaded the thought of having to work out an independent program. I needed to help him be a bit more presentable to his peers and wondered where the time and energy would come from to teach him.

For the first week or so, I observed Jamie Jon and began to establish good communication with him. I saw that his reading comprehension was about sixth-grade level, but with only literal comprehension. His math skills were nonexistent, although the previous school projected division. He had not a clue even what math meant. As stated, it was next to impossible to decipher his written work due to his motor difficulties, so I decided to let him lead me to what he could do. Finally, a plan emerged. I would need a paraprofessional to help me implement the new plan I had devised. First, he would be taught computers because waiting for him to get anything down on paper took forever. The process was long and tedious for him and for us. His aide would sit beside him as he learned keyboarding skills, guiding his hands and overseeing his practice. This would take practice and more practice. Then I would take over, and Jamie Jon would dictate his answers to me on his written assignments as we sat together at the computer.

Learning Disabilities: The Myth

Slowly, I found out that Jamie Jon loved reading, even though his comprehension was not so high, and he loved writing. I set up a program at the local library for him to shelve books for two hours a day with the supervision of the aide. There were many skills that he would learn such as filling out a time card, following directions, and alphabetizing. Of course, he would increase responsibility for himself and responsibilities on the job, and gain some independence. These skills were taught on a gradient with tight supervision and then supervision was faded slowly. One of the things I had to get him to extinguish was his self-stimulating habit of publicly rubbing his crotch. Eventually, he switched to rubbing his thigh. Whew! He was ready to go to work as far as I was concerned.

Jamie Jon would have two periods with me, the LI teacher, for reading and math, one period with the paraprofessional to work on keyboarding, and other classes in the regular curriculum. His program with math is described in detail in the chapter on math, so I will emphasize his writing here. I decided to have Jamie Jon sit beside me and dictate some of his writings, and boy, was I in for the surprise of my life. I sat down beside Jamie Jon and readied myself at the keyboard to type. By now, Jamie Jon had told me that he wrote a lot, and we had established a pretty solid communication pattern that followed a daily routine. He was comfortable with me and he would offer some comments.

"What do you write about?" I asked.

"Things I feel," he said flatly.

"Okay, so would you share with me?"

"Yes."

Thus, we began together: Jamie Jon dictating his illegible pieces to me at the computer. The most astounding but simple lines of poetry came from this boy who appeared to be devoid of feelings. He dictated and I typed. I saved every single piece of paper that he shared with me because I had hatched a plan. This boy would be published and in the school literary magazine! It was tricky, though, because both my sons were on the literary magazine staff: one was the editor and artist that year, the other a contributing writer and staff member. I knew how the selection process went; it was well publicized. Students submitted work that was assigned numbers after their names were removed. Then the work was evaluated by the literary staff members and assigned points. I decided that we must submit Jamie Jon's work anonymously so that my sons would not have to contend with comments about their mother's pushing to have a handicapped student's work published. This worked. He would submit through a third party and only sign with his first two initials so that it could not be traced at all.

Imagine our surprise and delight when two of JJ's pieces were selected and published. Unbeknownst to my son, he illustrated one of the pieces. My sons were in for a shock when I congratulated them on the quality of the magazine and said that I especially liked a couple of poems by JJ.

"Yeah, they were pretty good," my oldest son said, "but we don't know who it was."

"I do," I said. "It's Jamie Jon!"

"You're kidding!" my other son said.

"No! It's true!"

I decided then and there to present the copies of the literary magazine to Jamie Jon and his mother at the annual review that was coming up the next week. His mother burst into tears of joy when Jamie Jon read his poem "I Look to the Sea" to her from the magazine. His smile was four feet wide, appropriate for the first time ever that school year.

Bennie

"I like your legs, Mit Tunah [Ms. Turner]," Bennie said grinning. "Thank you, Bennie," I said. Bennie was a student with Down's syndrome who showed up one year at the American school in northern Italy. He was nearly eighteen years old and had begun to show a keen interest in the opposite sex. I had arrived from Sicily that year to set up a program for Bennie and another student with severe learning and behavior problems. Bennie had an IQ of about 45 on the Weschler Intelligence Test for Children and read on about the first-grade level. He had rudimentary language skills and could write his name and follow very simple directions. Setting up his program would be a challenge, and at the same time I wondered what would happen to him socially; he was the only retarded student

Learning Disabilities: The Myth

in the school. I was not prepared for what I would experience over the course of the next three years.

Bennie was one of those students that everybody just loved; at least they did in the beginning. He was friendly, smiled readily, and said hello to everyone in the halls and in his classes. The problem—and it was a big one—was where and with whom would he socialize, what kind of jobs could he learn, and what would I be able to teach him that would transfer to what he would be doing when he left high school. For certain, he was like a fish out of water.

At first, Bennie delighted the other students. He was their new toy, the cute retarded kid in school. I set up a program for Bennie as best I could, and so began our first year together. He had an aide assigned to him that would escort him everywhere except when he was with me. In three years, he had three different aides. Bennie did all right for a while when everything was new and he was receiving a lot of attention from everyone. The PE coach noticed that he could shoot baskets with tremendous accuracy, and, right away, he asked Bennie to be on the basketball team. I held my breath on this, knowing that he could not possibly understand plays and follow the directions during the heated excitement of a game, and I questioned the wisdom of such a move. The parents wanted it and that was that. Almost immediately, the news media was called in to film Bennie with the high school team shooting baskets. His parents and the coach were so proud, as was Bennie. He was instantly a celebrity! The film was shown on the six o'clock news!

Not too long after the excitement died down, Bennie was creating problems on the team because he could not follow the directions and pace of the game and was subsequently removed. The coach said he would give Bennie extra time during PE to work out with the basketball and team. That initiative faded immediately, and Bennie was left out, feeling rejected. About this time, Bennie was placed in an art class, but there was a whole lot of talk about art history and the drawing was complicated, and he could not do what the others were doing, even with sketching assignments. Soon he began creating a bit of a disturbance and had to be removed by his aide.

So now the only options for classes were physical education, though his participation was limited, and my classes. I set up a work experience with the Italian workers in our commissary. Though they could not speak English, they were able to work with him just fine as long as his aide was there. His job was stamping the price on the packages of vegetables. The Italian workers packaged and he stamped. This kept him happy for a while, and I thought at least he is doing something that is useful. In the meantime, I had my hands full with this other student.

During that first year, my oldest son became extremely ill and was eventually diagnosed with Burkitt's lymphoma, the fastest growing of all human cancers. He was in the final stages, though we did not know it at the time. I was new to this school and was immediately given additional duties of an administrative nature that took a lot of time. These duties and the responsibilities of setting up a new program kept me in the office late after the school day ended. I was also preparing for a federal monitoring. Both sons had adapted well to this environment, yet something was not right with the oldest one. Neither ever missed school, so I did not pay too much attention to what was going on. When I did realize something was wrong, my son was in dire pain, and I became desperate to find a diagnosis. Bennie sensed something was wrong, though I tried to hide it.

There was another problem: I was working for a very low-toned and sleazy principal, who eventually was put in jail following allegations of sexual molestation by some male students in the school, two of whom were my students. The students had agreed to be wired by the army's investigative wing and taped the principal's comments. Bennie was the light in my life at school during those dark days. He would look right into my eyes with those big, blue, almond-shaped eyes, and grinning at me would say, "It okay."

Before long, I had to leave Bennie to take my son to the States for chemotherapy and was gone for about two months. When I returned, Bennie was never quite the same. He had not understood that I would be coming back, I think. The program was not right for him anyway, and he started his decline. He was happy to see me but the joy in him was washed out totally. I could not quite reach him like I had always done. It saddened me, but I thought that he would bounce back. He did bounce back but in a way that I never expected. Not long after, he had a seizure-like episode in the library while he

Learning Disabilities: The Myth

was working with the speech teacher. She immediately called the ambulance and described his behavior to the hospital staff. Bennie was picked up by the ambulance with its lights flashing and the siren going full blast with students and staff congregating nearby.

Bennie found ways to be noticed, ways to be part of the group. He would no longer be ignored. One day Bennie was late coming to class in the morning because he was arresting students as they got off the bus. He was checking the students' identification cards and directing them. His brother had worked as a police officer in Los Angeles after leaving the military, and Bennie had "borrowed" his police badge. Now he was playing this game with the students. Most laughed and went along with him. Another time, Bennie was outside with the aide, walking back from his job, when he saw a group of soldiers jogging around the base for their physical exercise and took off after them. Two hours later, my aide was able to capture him and bring him back to school. He had mud and grass all over his shoes and pant legs, but this bothered him not in the least. He was grinning at me, "I back!" he announced. He had had quite a good time. My aide was exhausted!

Bennie was noticing girls more and more. He even had one picked out as his girlfriend. Most of the girls were quite tolerant of Bennie, and a couple of the girls showed him special attention. However, it began to get out of hand when the boyfriend of one of these girls became brutal in his remarks when he noticed that Bennie was calling his girl his girlfriend. "Get out of here, Retard!"

Bennie asked me later on, "Why I 'tarded?"

"I don't know, Bennie," I said.

"I not 'tarded!" Bennie said emphatically.

"Maybe we all are retarded in some ways, Bennie," I said.

I think this incident was the beginning of the end for Bennie. My son was still in the U.S., undergoing megadoses of chemotherapy, and I was back on the job, getting ready for the federal monitoring. I was trying my best to do my job with Bennie and Monty, as well as be a mother to my younger son. By now, we had changed principals, and this next one was a rough, loudmouthed man who had foaming-at-the-mouth fits in public if you crossed him in any way. On one of our walks one day, I told Bennie that all bad principals should be fired. Then we made a language game.

"What do you do to bad principals, Bennie?"

"Fire 'em, Mit Tunah, fire 'em!"

I felt enormously better after Bennie's agreement. There were times that I thought Bennie was the only one who understood me. For certain, I was the only one in the school who understood him. Both sons needed me, and the job was suppressive, not teaching Bennie and Monty, just everything else. Bennie and I had such an affinity for each other; I could sense his great spirit beyond the limitations of his mind.

Not long after Bennie's first seizure, he had another one, and I was called into the library where he had found an audience for this episode.

"Get up, Bennie," I said. "You get up right now, Bennie MacDougal!"

"Okay, Mit Tunah, I get up," said Bennie.

A few weeks later, Bennie had a seizure in the cafeteria, and the nurse was called in to check on him. She immediately called the hospital and ambulance. By the time I arrived, Bennie was being hauled away on a stretcher to the waiting ambulance. I could hear the sirens going as the ambulance headed for the hospital, and I could picture Bennie grinning from ear to ear. The next day, I visited him in the hospital and took him a magazine on Michael Jackson. Recently, Bennie had taken to wearing a glove on one hand like Jackson.

"Hurry up and come back, Bennie," I said, "I need you."

"Okay, Mit Tunah, I come back," Bennie said.

Sure enough, in a day or two, Bennie was back.

"I going on a love boat, Mit Tunah," said Bennie. This was Bennie's favorite show and he talked about it endlessly, if I would let him. I swore all he did at home was watch television and videos. I would ask Bennie his news each day when he and Monty would write their language reports. They would write about the weather, how they felt, and tell about their news. Bennie also would talk about the Night Stalker. The Night Stalker was a serial killer who was on the loose, and Bennie would watch the six o'clock news faithfully every day to find out where the Night Stalker might strike next. He

Learning Disabilities: The Myth

would bring in stories from the news but could only recall bits and pieces of one, and it always was the Night Stalker. So we would talk about the Night Stalker every day, just to learn straight language. And every day, I would try to help him extend it or get a new twist.

Bennie's so-called seizures increased in frequency over the next year, and I watched him go downhill gradually as he became more and more socially isolated. His parents expressed concern but not enough to sacrifice the father's career and return to the United States and back to California. In California, Bennie could have been enrolled in a sheltered workshop, had a social life, and learned skills for employment. "Bennie will be fine," his father said.

One day my aide came running to me all out of breath, and said, "Bennie has locked himself in a stall in the bathroom and won't come out!" I immediately got the assistance of a male student to go in and clear the way before I went in. Bennie had refused to obey anyone.

"You come out of there right this minute, Bennie MacDougal!" I said in a very firm voice. Silence. "You come out, Bennie MacDougal, or I am coming in to get you right now!"

"Okay, Mit Tunah, I come," said Bennie

In the third year, it was time for graduation, and I had to arrange Bennie's graduation plan. I convinced the parents that Bennie could graduate with a certificate. That was fine with them, only they wanted all the pomp and circumstance of graduation. This meant cap, gown, onstage, and all the rest. I just prayed that Bennie would do it without a scene. My oldest son would also be on that same stage, and I wanted to enjoy his ceremony because only two years before the doctors had given little hope that he would ever see this day. So Bennie and my son would be on the same stage in the fifteenth-century opera house in the city where I worked. This was great, only I did not like what I would have to do to bring Bennie to this point. "Certificates are not allowed in this school system," the principal said coldly, "only diplomas." What did I do? I was *required* to create a lie—a lie that said Bennie had all the credentials to meet the graduation requirements. I falsified that he had completed courses in U.S. history, world history, algebra, and all the rest of the necessary high school curriculum. To no avail, I pleaded with the principal and my coordinator of special education, saying that this was wrong. What did this lie do to the idea of the diploma for my son? And others? The special education law and those interpreting it had gone haywire. This was not the intent of the law!

Bennie did graduate, and Bennie did behave himself for me, I am convinced. We drilled and drilled, and he walked across the stage and shook hands and accepted his diploma just like my son and all the others. I pictured Bennie wadding up that diploma at the first chance he got and ringing the nearest trash can. He looked at me with those big, blue, almond-shaped eyes and grinned from ear to ear as I congratulated him.

"Got it, Mit Tunah!" Bennie said as he waved the diploma. If his parents had not arrived at that very moment, I knew that diploma was a goner.

To order books and for additional information on Study Technology and Communication courses contact:

Applied Scholastics International
11755 Riverview Drive
St Louis, MO 63138
http://www.appliedscholastics.org

Printed in the United States
35065LVS00004B/7-12